A Ray

REINHARD HEYDRICH, L.. AND THE NORTH STAFFORDSHIRE MINERS

Russell Phillips

Shilka Publishing
www.shilka.co.uk

Shilka Publishing
Apt 2049
Chynoweth House
Trevissome Park
Truro
TR4 8UN
www.shilka.co.uk

Book Layout ©2013
BookDesignTemplates.com

Ordering Information:
Quantity sales. Special discounts are available on quantity purchases by corporations, associations, and others. For details, contact the "Special Sales Department" at the address above.

A Ray of Light/ Russell Phillips. —1st ed.
ISBN 978-0-9955133-0-3

Contents

Dedicated to my dad, Horace.

"The miner's lamp dispels the shadows on the coal face. It can also send a ray of light across the sea to those who struggle in darkness"

—Dr Barnett Stross

Preface

In March 2013, I was at the Potteries Museum in Stoke-on-Trent with my son. We were asked if we'd like to see a film about the village of Lidice, destroyed by the Nazis during the Second World War. I didn't know the story of Lidice, and assumed it would be similar to that of Oradour-sur-Glane in France, the site of an infamous massacre.

The film showed that Reinhard Heydrich, a senior Nazi and one of the main architects of the Holocaust, was assassinated in 1942. In retribution, the men of Lidice were shot, the women and children were sent to an extermination camp, and the buildings were destroyed. So far, the story was depressingly similar to that of Oradour-sur-Glane, although differing in detail.

The story didn't end there, and so the film continued. The buildings were bulldozed. The rubble was taken away. The remains in the cemetery were dug up. The stream that ran through the village was rerouted. The area was landscaped. When they were finished, there was no sign that a village had ever been there. This was exactly what Hitler had ordered. The destruction of the village and the murder of its inhabitants weren't enough; he wanted the memory of Lidice to die. It was to be as if the village had never existed.

After the viewing, I spoke to Nicola Winstanley, one of the artists of the Unearthed 2013 project. She told me the remarkable story of what happened next. How the generosity of North Staffordshire's miners meant that Lidice was rebuilt after the war. Hitler died, but in direct opposition to his orders, Lidice lives.

It is my sincere hope that this short book will help spread the story of Lidice and North Staffordshire's miners. It's an incredible story of outrageous cruelty, but also of tremendous compassion and generosity. We should remember the atrocity. It is when we forget these things that we allow them to happen again. We should also remember the miners and their wonderful generosity. They showed us that humans can be good and kind, as well as cruel. Let us remember their story as an inspiration and example to ourselves and our children.

Russell Phillips
Stoke-on-Trent, June 2016

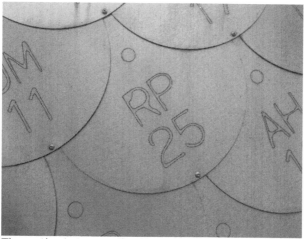

The author's tag on the Unearthed sculpture

Acknowledgements

In the UK, the story of Stoke-on-Trent's connection to Lidice was forgotten for many years, lost to the expediencies of Cold War politics. Alan Gerrard discovered the story in 2010. Since then, he and his wife Cheryl have worked to restore that memory. Alan gracefully agreed to check this manuscript for factual errors.

Nicola Winstanley and Sarah Nadin are the artists who created the Unearthed sculpture. In the months before the sculpture was unveiled, they worked to raise awareness of the 'Lidice Shall Live' campaign.

It is through the efforts of these people that I and others became aware of the Lidice story. Without them, this book would not exist. I offer grateful thanks to them for the work that they have done to spread awareness of the story.

Elizabeth Carver provided invaluable help improving the initial manuscript, making it a much better read.

Any errors or omissions in the final book, however, are my own.

Reinhard Heydrich

Reinhard Heydrich was born on 7th March 1904. A persistent, though untrue rumour held that his father was Jewish. After being widowed, Heydrich's grandmother had married a man named Süss. Süss wasn't Jewish, but it was a common name among Jews, leading many to assume that he had Jewish ancestry. Even before the Nazis rose to power, anti-Semitism was rife in Germany. Consequently, the rumour caused problems for the Heydrich family.

In 1919, the fifteen-year-old Heydrich joined the Märacker Freikorps, a right-wing paramilitary group formed to fight against revolutionaries. Later, he and his father joined the Halle volunteers, a home defence group. Heydrich also joined the nationalist and anti-Semitic Deutscher Schutz und Trutzbund.

In March 1922, Heydrich joined the navy as an officer cadet. Unfortunately for him, another cadet from Halle passed on the rumour of his Jewish ancestry. This earned him the nickname "blond Moses". Despite this, he secured promotion and received good reports. He worked in signals and learned English, French, and Russian.

In 1923 and 1924, Heydrich served on the SMS Berlin, where Wilhelm Canaris was the first officer. The two men struck up a friendship, and Heydrich was a frequent guest at Canaris' house. Heydrich appeared to be set on a future in the navy. By the time he proposed to his future wife, Lina von Osten, in December 1930, he had been promoted to first lieutenant.

The German navy had very strict codes of conduct for its officers. In 1931, Heydrich was brought before a court of honour to face charges of breach of promise, brought by an ex-girlfriend. He claimed that she had arrived at his rooms one night, asking for lodging. According to Heydrich, she had stayed the night, but nothing had happened between them. The prosecution held that Heydrich had invited her to his rooms because of the expense of hotels. She had agreed out of necessity, but resisted his advances.

Although Lina believed Heydrich, the court found against him, and he was discharged in April 1931. He appealed, but the court's decision was upheld. He was deeply upset by the loss of his career and standing as an officer and a gentleman. It also affected his personal relationships. His mother blamed Lina, and the relationship between the two women never recovered. Heydrich had gone from a promising career in the navy to having no prospects, and Lina's parents withdrew their consent for marriage. Lina refused to break off the engagement, although the wedding had to wait until Heydrich secured employment.

Lina and her parents were members of the Nazi party, and Heydrich also joined in June 1931. Himmler, the head of the SS, was planning a counter-intelligence division. A friend of the von Osten family secured an interview for Heydrich. Himmler was impressed, and Heydrich started his new job on 1st August. He showed a talent for the work, quickly building up a network of spies and informants, which led to rapid promotion. In December 1931, he married Lina and was promoted to Sturmbannführer (major) as a wedding gift from Himmler.

Within a few months of the wedding, rumours of Heydrich's Jewish ancestry surfaced again. Some of his previous Navy colleagues told the Gauleiter (regional party leader) in Halle that Heydrich's real name was Süss, and that he had Jewish ancestry. The Gauleiter dutifully reported the accusation to Nazi party headquarters. An investigation was launched into the Heydrich family, which concluded that they were "free from any coloured or Jewish blood". Nonetheless, the rumours persisted. Wilhelm Canaris even claimed to have copies of documents proving Heydrich's Jewish ancestry, though he never produced them.

In spite of these attempts to discredit him, Heydrich's career continued to progress. In July 1932 Himmler promoted him to Standartenführer (colonel) and appointed him head of the SS security service, the SD (Sicherheitsdienst). In July 1933 Heydrich's first child, Klaus, was born. Himmler and Ernst Röhm, the head of the SA (the Nazi party's paramilitary wing, known as "Brownshirts"), were the child's godfathers.

1934 saw the Nazi party split by internal power struggles. Ernst Röhm was gaining power. His desire to have his SA replace the regular army caused anger and resentment among the regular armed forces, and was directly opposed by Hitler. Members of the Nazi party started aligning themselves with one faction or the other. At this time, Himmler's SS was an integral part of the SA. Himmler and Heydrich worked together to separate the SS from the SA. They wanted to transform the SS from its original function as a bodyguard force into an elite, independent corps.

Things came to a head in June 1934, by which time Heydrich was head of the Gestapo, the Nazi secret police. Hitler discovered that President Hindenburg was considering a declaration of martial law because of the threat from the SA. To avoid this, Hitler ordered Himmler and Heydrich to work against Röhm. Despite Röhm being a godfather to Heydrich's son, the two men compiled a dossier of fake evidence against him. This purportedly showed that France had paid Röhm to depose Hitler, and that the SA was to be used to launch a coup. At the end of June 1934, the SS and Gestapo arrested and executed many of Hitler's opponents, during what became known as the Night of the Long Knives. This included many senior members of the SA, including Röhm. Röhm was locked in a cell with a pistol, and told that if he didn't shoot himself, his captors would do it for him. A defiant Röhm refused, saying "If I am to be killed, let Adolf do it himself". When he didn't shoot himself within the ten minutes given him, his captors shot him in his cell.

The purges carried out during the Night of the Long Knives extended beyond the SA. Political opponents, critics, and old enemies of the Nazi party were also arrested. This included Vice-Chancellor Papen, despite his repeated protests that he could not be legally arrested. Many of those arrested were executed, some brutally. Papen was released on Hitler's orders, but he never again criticised the Nazi party.

The SA itself survived, but became a sporting organisation. Many within Germany, including most of the army, were happy to see the SA so thoroughly gutted. President Hindenburg even sent a congratulatory telegram to Hitler, expressing "profoundly felt gratitude" at Hitler's "nipping treason in the bud". Some Germans, including some army officers, didn't believe the Nazi claims of treason. The scale of the massacre and the ever-increasing reach of the Gestapo, however, meant that very few spoke out.

Heydrich worked with Himmler to increase the size and influence of the Gestapo, and in 1936, the Gestapo Law

Heydrich, ca 1940/41

(Bundesarchiv, CC-BY-SA)

came into force. This allowed the Gestapo
to act outside the law, as long as it was
carrying out the leadership's will. This
effectively meant that they could
arbitrarily arrest, imprison, or even kill
anyone. No evidence was needed, and
there was no judicial oversight.

In 1938, Heydrich played a leading role
in the organisation of Kristallnacht
(Crystal Night), when thousands of Jewish
buildings, including schools and hospitals,
were attacked. Around 30,000 Jews were
sent to concentration camps. In 1939, he

helped to plan Operation Himmler, a series of fake attacks on German border buildings. These "unprovoked attacks" served as the pretext for the German invasion of Poland. In January 1942, Heydrich chaired the infamous Wannsee Conference, where he outlined his "final solution of the Jewish question". The conference worked out the logistical details involved in running the death camps of the Holocaust.

By 1942, Heydrich was firmly established as a senior member of the Nazi party, and counted both Himmler and Hitler as personal friends. Arguably the most evil of the senior Nazis, Hitler referred to him as "the man with the iron heart". The Czechs had other names for him, such as "Hangman Heydrich" and "The Butcher of Prague".

The Reich Protectorate of Bohemia and Moravia

In 1938, Britain and France signed the Munich Agreement, allowing Germany to seize part of Czechoslovakia. Six months later, in March 1939, Slovakia declared independence and allied itself with Germany, which immediately recognised the new state. The next day, German armies marched into the remainder of Czechoslovakia. Having already lost most of their border, the Czechs were unable to resist. Some areas were annexed by Hungary and Poland,

and the remainder became the Reich
Protectorate of Bohemia and Moravia.
Resistance groups were formed to fight
the occupiers, and the former president
Dr Edvard Beneš set up a government in
exile. Czech soldiers set up armed forces
abroad, the first being formed in Cracow,
Poland in April 1939. After Poland
surrendered to Germany that September,
Czechs fought in the French and British
armed forces.

By 1941, the Germans were becoming
concerned about the level of resistance in
the protectorate. Hitler believed that the
Reich Protector, Konstantin von Neurath,
was too lenient. When von Neurath fell ill
in September, he was sent away,
ostensibly to recuperate. Reinhard
Heydrich, newly promoted to SS-
Obergruppenführer and General of Polizei,
became the new Reich Protector.

Heydrich arrived in Prague on 27th
September 1941, and immediately set to
work. The prime minister and minister of
traffic, General Alois Eliáš and Jiří Havelka,
were arrested the same day. Martial law
was introduced, under which the courts

had three options: they could sentence the accused to death, hand them over to the Gestapo, or declare them innocent. Sentences were to be carried out immediately, with no chance of appeal.

It is believed that over 400 people were executed in the three months following Heydrich's arrival. Thousands more were arrested and sent to concentration camps. The charges included subversion, sabotage, membership of a political party, or simply listening to foreign radio broadcasts. The camp at Osvětím became notorious for the particularly barbaric treatment Czechs received there.

Heydrich presided over a conference on the "final solution to the Jewish problem" in the protectorate on 10th October. He stated that there were around 88,000 Jews in the protectorate, 48,000 of them in Prague. A decision was made to build a temporary collection camp at Terezín. The plan was to send two or three trains, each holding around 1,000 people, every day. Synagogues and other Jewish places of prayer were closed. Some Czechs had shown support to the Jews, wearing the

Star of David as an act of solidarity. The police were ordered to put such people into protective custody. 93,942 Jews were deported from the protectorate during the war. Fewer than 4,000 survived.

In a counterpoint to his brutal oppression, Heydrich improved conditions for workers. The armaments factories, which made a significant contribution to the German war effort, were treated particularly well. He worked with the National Centre of the Employees' Union (NOUZ). Several luxury hotels were converted into recreation facilities for workers, while food rations, social insurance, and annuities were increased. These measures helped to win over some of the protectorate's working class, especially those who worked in munitions factories and saw the greatest benefits.

In January 1942, a new government was inaugurated. The new prime minister promised that the protectorate would work hard for a final German victory. In return, martial law was lifted in Prague and Brno, and some students were released from concentration camps.

Particular emphasis was placed on the production of military equipment. Over 100,000 workers were removed from "unsuitable" jobs and moved to work that would help the war effort. From December 1941, Czechs could be conscripted to work anywhere in the Reich.

In Britain, the Allies were concerned by the acceptance of a pro-German government. There seemed to be little resistance to Heydrich and the German occupation. The Czech government-in-exile had been recognised by the British in June 1941. Despite this, the 1938 Munich Agreement, which had ceded the Sudetenland area to Germany, was still valid. The Czech government, wanting the pre-war boundaries restored after the war, was desperate to persuade the Allies to renounce the agreement. They needed to do something dramatic, and the decision was made to assassinate either Reinhard Heydrich or Karl Herman Frank, Heydrich's deputy and state secretary. It was believed that assassinating either man would be a valid act of retribution for the brutal treatment of the Czechs. Such an operation would prove the resolve of the local population, and improve the government's standing in London. It would also send a strong message to the Nazis, demonstrating that even their highest-ranking members were not safe. The operation was code-named Anthropoid, and was planned for Czechoslovakia's Independence Day, on 28th October.

Operation Anthropoid

In 1941 the Czech government-in-exile had formed "Special Group D" of the Ministry of Defence, which trained soldiers to perform intelligence collection and sabotage in occupied Czechoslovakia. In this regard, it had a lot in common with the British Special Operations Executive (SOE). Special Group D were trained in parachuting and guerrilla warfare techniques at Special Training Schools (STS) set up by the SOE. An assassination was exactly the type of mission that was envisioned when Special Group D was set up.

In October, Special Group D and the SOE began planning Heydrich's assassination, under the code name Operation Anthropoid. Warrant Officer Jozef Gabčík and Staff Sergeant Karel Svoboda were chosen for the operation, and sent to Manchester for parachute training. Svoboda suffered a head injury during a training jump and had to be replaced by Warrant Officer Jan Kubiš, delaying the start of the operation.

Multiple Czech resistance groups had been in radio contact with London from 1939, and in 1940 had consolidated under the leadership of the Home Resistance Headquarters (ÚVOD). During 1941 the Germans discovered many of the transmitters, severing the links. By July, there was only a single transmitter operating, and so Operation Percentage was set up to create new radio links. On the night of 3rd/4th October 1941, Lance Corporal František Pavelka parachuted into Czechoslovakia. He carried equipment to set up a new radio link. This included a radio transmitter, crystals, new encryption keys, and other apparatus.

Agonisingly for the Allies, all contact was lost with the Czech resistance on the very night that Operation Percentage was launched, when the Gestapo found the remaining transmitter. Soon after, the Gestapo arrested almost all of the ÚVOD resistance organisation's leaders. Lance Corporal Pavelka was caught and interrogated. It was during this interrogation that the village of Lidice was first mentioned in connection with the Czech resistance.

With communication between Czechoslovakia and Britain now cut, the Silver programme received priority over Operation Anthropoid. The Silver programme consisted of two groups equipped with communications equipment, who were parachuted into Czechoslovakia to re-establish communications with Britain. Initial reports from Silver indicated that the Czech resistance would be reorganised, following the arrest of its leaders, by the end of March 1942.

Operation Anthropoid was postponed until radio links were re-established, and so Gabčík and Kubiš used the time to improve their planning and attend special

Gabčík and Kubiš

SOE courses. In Scotland, they attended a course to improve their shooting and grenade throwing. Particular emphasis was placed on instinctive shooting in action and in situations likely to be encountered while operating in occupied territory. They then moved to Station XVII in Brickendonbury Manor, near London, where they trained in the use of explosives, various types of fuses, and creating booby traps. In particular, they were trained in the use of special bombs made from modified No. 73 anti-tank grenades and fitted with sensitive contact fuses. It was to be one of these "special bombs" that would be used in the assassination of Heydrich. At Villa Bellasis near Dorking, they improved their driving skills, use of Morse code, and orientation in unknown territory. They practised procedures after landing, marking drop zones for supply aircraft, shooting, and throwing hand grenades.

On 1st December 1941, Gabčík and Kubiš each signed the following pledge:

> *"The substance of my mission basically is that I will be sent back to my homeland, with another member of the Czechoslovak Army, in order to commit an act of sabotage or terrorism at a place and in a situation depending on our findings at the given site and under the given circumstances, and I will do so effectively so as to generate the sought-after response not only in the home country but also abroad. I will do it to the extent of my best knowledge and conscience so that I can successfully fulfil this mission for which I have volunteered."*

On 28th December 1941, two months later than originally planned, the two men boarded the RAF Halifax bomber that would fly them to their home country of Czechoslovakia. Despite being intercepted by fighters twice, the aircraft managed to continue the operation. Heavy snow cover made navigation difficult, leading the crew to mistake Pilsen (where they were shot at by an anti-aircraft battery) for Prague. Consequently, at 02:24 the two men parachuted down near Nehvizdy, east of Prague, about 50 miles away from the planned landing point. On the return journey, the Halifax was fired upon twice more by anti-aircraft batteries, but landed safely at 08:19 on 29th December.

Unsurprisingly, the Luftwaffe had monitored the bomber's flight over Czechoslovakia. They informed Heydrich that paratroopers had almost certainly been dropped at some point during the flight. Wehrmacht units searched the areas of the flight. Police were ordered to search for suspicious persons who had arrived in the protectorate on or since 29th December 1941.

Gabčík and Kubiš hid their equipment in a garden shed where they spent the night, and discovered in the morning that they had been dropped in the wrong area. They headed to Pilsen to find the resistance contacts that they had been given. These contacts provided Gabčík with medical treatment for an injury he'd sustained in the parachute drop. In Prague, contact was made with anti-German organisations, which helped with hideout flats and other preparations for the attack. The equipment that they'd brought with them was hidden in various locations around Prague.

Once Gabčík's injuries had healed, the two men started monitoring Heydrich, watching his movements, and began to plan the assassination. In April, they carried out a secondary mission, working with other parachutists to guide British bombers to the Škoda armaments factory in Pilsen. This factory was a major source of military equipment for Germany, and four failed attempts had already been made to bomb it. On the night of 25th April, Gabčík, Kubiš, and others set fire to two barns to guide the British bombers to the factory. Cloud covered the target, and once again, the bombing mission was a failure, with no bombs landing on the factory.

Assassination

In April 1942, Heydrich moved from his temporary quarters in Prague Castle to a château in Panenské Břežany. Lina, always conscious of status, was delighted to be living in a château, and spent a good deal of money and slave labour improving the building with new bathrooms and a swimming pool. This move also gave the attackers an opportunity, and a plan was devised. He would be attacked during his daily commute to Prague Castle. The local resistance were not told what was planned, but they had worked it out for themselves. Fearing major reprisals, they sent a message to Britain. They wanted the cancellation of any plan to assassinate Heydrich, warning that "This assassination would not help the Allies and would bring immense consequences upon our nation". Instead, they suggested that a local quisling be targeted, with Emanuel Moravec named as the first choice. A reply was received two days later. The operation was to go ahead.

Himmler was already concerned about the possibility of an attempt on Heydrich's life. He had ordered a company of SS guards to be quartered in the village, outside the château grounds. Heydrich disliked the presence of the guards, believing that any protection was tantamount to an admission of fear, and therefore damaging to German prestige. He flatly refused to take an escort when driving, and drove in an open-topped car with only his driver accompanying him.

On 27th May, Heydrich was driven from the château to his office at Prague Castle, as usual. Gabčík and Kubiš, having studied the route that Heydrich habitually took, were waiting for him. They were positioned at a tight curve, where the car would be forced to slow down. A third man, Valčik, acted as lookout, roughly 100m away.

Shortly after 10:30, the car approached, and Gabčík stepped out into the road to open fire. His Sten sub-machine gun jammed. Heydrich, sat in the front right seat, ordered his driver, SS-Oberscharführer Johannes Klein, to stop the car. Heydrich stood up to fire back at Gabčík. Kubiš threw a bomb into the car, but his aim was off, and the bomb landed outside the car, in front of the right rear wheel. Heydrich, Kubiš, and a bystander were wounded by shrapnel. A large piece of metal was lodged in Heydrich's left lower back. Although in considerable pain, he was still able to move.

Both attackers thought that they had failed in their mission, neither realising that Heydrich was wounded. Kubiš pedalled away on his bicycle, with Heydrich following him, unable to walk in a straight line due to his wound. Heydrich tried to fire, but his pistol misfired. Weak from shock, he quickly gave up the chase, and ordered Klein to chase Gabčík.

Gabčík had hidden in a butcher's shop, but the shopkeeper, a Nazi sympathiser, ran out into the road and shouted to Klein. Realising there was no rear exit, Gabčík ran out of the front door, colliding with Klein. Gabčík fired, hitting Klein in the leg, and ran. Klein ordered the shopkeeper to take his gun and go after Gabčík, but the shopkeeper only went a few yards before giving up.

Gabčík and Kubiš managed to make their way to a pair of safe houses in Prague. Kubiš had suffered a head wound from the bomb explosion, and was treated by Dr Břetislav Lyčka. Lyčka was a member of JINDRA, one of the Czech resistance groups, and had previously helped the two men.

Heydrich had staggered back to the car and collapsed against the bonnet. A Czech woman recognised him and shouted for a car to take him to hospital. A delivery lorry was flagged down, and the driver was persuaded to take Heydrich to the emergency room at Bulovka Hospital. Heydrich arrived there shortly after 11:00, and was admitted under the registration number 12.555/42. He had suffered a fractured rib, a left pneumothorax, and major damage to the diaphragm and spleen. His lower left back was bleeding profusely. He was initially examined by Dr Snadjr, who immediately called for Dr W. Dick, the chief of surgery.

Dr Dick arrived with a number of German surgeons and examined the wound. Initially believing that it could be operated on under local anaesthetic in the minor surgery room, he nonetheless ordered a radiograph. This showed that the injuries would actually require major surgery under a general anaesthetic. Heydrich refused, and insisted on a surgeon from Berlin. Dr Dick repeated that the operation was urgent, and offered to call Professor J. Hohlbaum, a Silesian German and chairman of the surgery department at the local Charles V University. After some deliberation, Heydrich agreed, and Hohlbaum was called.

Moved to the operating theatre, Heydrich was silent and aloof, to the point of ignoring the anaesthetist's questions about loose teeth and dentures. He did allow the anaesthetist to examine his mouth, and was put under general anaesthetic without any problems. The operation started at around noon and lasted about an hour. Professor Hohlbaum arrived while doctors Dick and Slalina were scrubbing. In his haste, he had forgotten his glasses. He told Dr Dick to begin, and that he would assist while an aide was sent for his glasses. Blood transfusions were administered at the start and end of the operation, and Heydrich was given tetanus and gas gangrene anti-toxins.

Dr Dick debrided the chest wound, resected the tip of the fractured rib, inserted a catheter, and closed the wound over the re-inflated left lung. Professor Hohlbaum took over, his glasses having arrived. However, as he was making an incision, Dr Dick noticed that he was sweating profusely. He quietly whispered, "Professor Hohlbaum, you are not well, allow me to take over". Dr Dick finished the procedure, assisted by Hohlbaum and Dr Slalina. The peritoneal cavity was filled with blood from the spleen, but the left kidney and other abdominal organs were undamaged. Dr Dick removed the damaged spleen, an 8x8cm piece of shrapnel, and a large quantity of car upholstery. He sutured the pancreatic tail, inserted a peritoneal drain, and closed the abdomen. Heydrich showed no signs of distress during the surgery, and his vital signs remained normal. Dr Dick provided post-operative care until 29th May, when SS physicians arrived and took over.

Once the operation was complete, Heydrich was moved to Dr Dick's office, which had been converted for use as a private room. He remained in this room until his death. Heydrich's wife Lina visited him early that afternoon, as he was waking from his anaesthetic.

Czech police had informed the Gestapo of the attack at around 10:45 that morning, but gave no details. Reports of attacks on Germans were common, and often false alarms, so the report was ignored for some time. They eventually discovered Heydrich in Bulovka Hospital as he was being prepared for surgery.

Shocked to discover the Reich Protector alone and without a guard, they immediately called for an SS squad to be dispatched to the hospital. Heydrich's floor was emptied of patients, with SS guards in their place. Machine guns were mounted on the roof, guards posted at entrances, and windows whitewashed to prevent sniper attack.

Reichsführer-SS Heinrich Himmler was notified immediately. He dispatched his personal physician and professor of orthopaedics in Berlin, Dr Karl Gebhardt, to take over Heydrich's care. Gebhardt, his assistant Dr L. Stumpfegger, and F. Sauerbruch, a renowned surgeon, arrived on the evening of 27th May. Himmler took a close interest in Heydrich's progress, receiving telephone updates from Gebhardt twice a day.

Other high-ranking Nazi officials reacted with fear and anger that an assassination attempt had been made on one of their own. Hitler demanded that the killers be found, and the Gestapo began arresting and interrogating thousands of people in a desperate attempt to find the men responsible.

The local nurses and pharmacists noted that large quantities of morphine were ordered for Heydrich. They even speculated that there may have been an addict among the physicians treating him. The dosages are unknown, but it is by no means certain that it was not all for Heydrich. If Gebhardt was trying to keep him comfortable during the frequent visits from his wife, Himmler, and SS colleagues, large quantities would have been needed.

Heydrich soon developed a fever and had copious wound drainage. Despite this, Gebhardt refused to give approval for a second operation. In the early hours of 3rd June, Gebhardt reported to Himmler that both the fever and wound drainage had improved and that Heydrich was recovering. Around noon on 3rd June, Heydrich was sitting in bed eating a late breakfast. Suddenly, he went into shock, possibly caused by septicaemia or cerebral embolism, and lapsed into a deep coma from which he never recovered. He died at 04:30 on 4th June. The cause of death was recorded as "gunshot wound/murder attempt/wound infection".

A post-mortem was carried out at noon on 4th June. The initial report was signed later that day. A longer report, including microscopic and bacteriological findings, was completed on 17th June. Both reports found that death was caused by virulent microbes or their toxins, with no evidence of chemical poisoning or surgical error.

On 6th June, a torch-lit procession took Heydrich's coffin to Prague Castle, where it was exhibited to the public the next day. The coffin was then taken to Berlin by train, and a ceremony was held in the new Reich Chancellery on 9th June. This was attended by many high-ranking Nazis, including Hitler, who placed Heydrich's decorations on his funeral pillow. The coffin was buried in Berlin's Invalidenfriedhof, although the exact location is not known. Hitler wanted a monumental tomb, but this was never built.

In October 1942, Himmler sent a letter of thanks to Heydrich's surgeons, which praised Gebhardt for easing his suffering. Gebhardt was later promoted to SS Major General and Supreme SS Physician, and received the Knight's Cross with Diamonds.

There have been rumours that botulinum toxins were planted in the grenade that was used in the attack, but there are no records to support such a claim. Neither Heydrich nor Kubiš, both wounded by the grenade, showed any symptoms of botulism. Botulinum toxins are fragile, and if any were deposited in the grenade, it is highly unlikely that they would have survived the long, cold flight, months of winter weather, and the heat of the explosion.

Reprisals

On 27th May, K. H. Frank, Heydrich's deputy, declared a state of civil emergency and imposed a curfew in the protectorate. His proclamation stated that "Anyone harbouring the culprits or having knowledge as to their identity or their whereabouts and failing to report it, will be shot with all his family."

Later that day, Himmler sent Frank a teleprinter message ordering the arrest that day of "the entire Czech intelligentsia among the first 10,000 hostages". Furthermore, the "first 100 most important adversaries among the Czech intelligentsia" were to be shot that evening. A massive search operation was initiated, in which 21,000 men searched 36,000 houses.

Reports of the reprisals reached Britain, and on 29th May the Czech government-in-exile released a statement. The statement condemned the reprisals in the strongest terms, calling them "… an act of brutality unique in history". The statement said that the Germans were "… calling down upon themselves just retribution in accordance with the Commandments of God and Man." President Beneš was confident that reprisals would not break the will of the Czech people. Rather, he believed that they would lead to an uprising against the German occupation and increased resistance.

Beneš' confidence was misplaced. On 2nd June, a public meeting was held in the Old Town Square in Prague. 60,000 people attended to hear the government denounce Heydrich's assassination and proclaim allegiance to the Third Reich.

In total, at least 5,000 people, including 3,000 Jews from the Terezín ghetto, were murdered in retaliation for Heydrich's death. To Beneš' disbelief, the Czech population did not resist. Heydrich's assassination earned acclaim and admiration from the Allies. Among the Czechs, there was recrimination and guilt over the cost in innocent lives.

On 3rd June, a letter addressed to Anna Maruščáková arrived at the factory where she worked in Slaný. She was off sick, so the factory owner opened the letter. It read:

> "*Dear Annie, excuse me for writing you so late, but maybe you'll understand, because you know that I have many worries. What I wanted to do, I have done. On the fatal day, I slept somewhere in Čabárna. I'm fine, I'll see you this week, and then we will never see each other again. Milan.*"

The factory owner had no idea what the message meant, but the cryptic nature of it made him suspicious. He contacted the German authorities, and Maruščáková was arrested that day. By this time, 157 people had been executed in reprisals for the attack on Heydrich. The assassins still had not been found, and the authorities were getting desperate. They had no idea who they were or where to find them.

Under interrogation, the young woman revealed that two men from a village named Lidice were in Britain, fighting for the Allies. The Gestapo knew that men had been parachuted into the protectorate the previous December. They concluded, erroneously, that these two men had been among the paratroopers, and that they had taken part in the attack on Heydrich. Orders were immediately issued to arrest their families. The fate of Lidice was sealed.

The letter writer, Vaclav Říha, was arrested and interrogated the next day. It soon became clear that he had no involvement in the resistance. In fact, he'd been having an affair with Maruščáková, and he wanted to end it. The letter had been deliberately vague to imply that he was in the resistance, and provide him with an excuse to end the affair. It became clear that this lead was actually a red herring, and that Lidice had no connection to Heydrich's death. Maruščáková, Říha, and the arrested family members were executed later that year.

The two men that Maruščáková had mentioned were Josef Horak and Josef Stříbrný. They were lieutenants in the RAF, still in Britain and blissfully unaware of the events unfolding around their home. None of this would save Lidice. Hitler was furious at the death of his friend, and he wanted to strike out. The small Czech village had been chosen as the target of his vengeance, and even though it was now clear that it was simply the victim of a terrible coincidence, this wasn't enough to save it. Hitler was so furious, he didn't just want to destroy Lidice; he wanted to destroy the memory of Lidice.

The Destruction of Lidice

Late at night on 9th June, the mining village of Lidice was surrounded by men of the Ordnungspolizei (Order Police) and SD. They were commanded by Horst Böhme, the Sicherheitspolizei (security police) chief. The villagers didn't see any reason to be overly concerned. No one was allowed to leave the village, but men returning home from the coal mines were allowed back in.

At about 07:00 the next morning, the women and children were taken to the village school. Men aged fifteen or over were taken to the Horák family's farm on the outskirts of the village. Mattresses were lined up against an outside wall, and then the men were taken outside, five at a time. They were lined up against the wall and shot. The dead were left where they fell, and as each new group of men came out, they had to stand in front of the bodies. As the pile of bodies grew, the firing squad had to periodically step back to keep their distance from the victims. After a while, Böhme decided that the executions were taking too long, and ordered the men to be shot in groups of ten. The shooting finally ended that afternoon. Nine men and two boys who were not in the village at the time were later executed in Prague. While the men were being executed, each of the village buildings were set ablaze. When the fires had died down, the remains of the buildings were destroyed with explosives.

The women and children of Lidice were taken to the grammar school at nearby

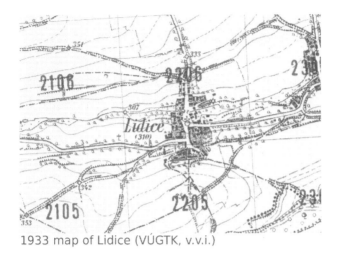

1933 map of Lidice (VÚGTK, v.v.i.)

Kladno, and kept there for three days. Four pregnant women had their foetuses forcibly aborted before being sent to extermination camps. The remaining women were taken to the camp at Ravensbrück, where they were forced to work in leather processing, road building, textile, and ammunition factories. Some women managed to survive, partly because other camp inmates helped frustrate efforts by the camp authorities to isolate the Lidice women.

The children were taken to Łódź in Poland, where they were given minimal care and no medical attention. Not surprisingly, they suffered from illness and a lack of hygiene. A few children were chosen for Germanisation and adopted by SS families. They were raised as Germans, and never told of their past or ancestry.

The next day, units of the Reich Work Forces (Reichsarbeitsdienst, commonly abbreviated to RAD) arrived to complete the destruction. There was to be no trace left, nothing to indicate that this was once the site of a village.

Anything that was still standing was bulldozed. The remains in the town cemetery were dug up and destroyed. The course of the stream that ran through the centre of the village was changed. Trees were felled and the village pond was filled in. The rubble was cleared from the site and the area was landscaped. All that remained was a solitary sapling, a pear tree. To complete the eradication, the name of the village was removed from official records, and maps showing the village were destroyed.

Unlike other massacres, the razing of Lidice was publicly and proudly announced to the world. Prague radio broadcast an announcement about the massacre. A report was issued, which claimed,

> *"In the course of the search for the murderers of SS Obergruppenführer Heydrich unmistakable indications were discovered that the population of the commune of Lidice near Kladno had afforded support and help to the set of culprits in question. Proofs were secured without the assistance of the local population, although enquiries were instituted among them. Their attitude towards the outrage which thus revealed itself, was aggravated by further acts hostile to the Reich, such, for example, as the discovery of treasonable printed matter, stores of arms and munitions, illegal wireless transmitters, and extremely large quantities of goods amenable to rationing, as well as the circumstances that the inhabitants of this commune are in the active service of enemies abroad".*

This, of course, was completely untrue, but it did serve to offer some level of justification for the atrocity. The German newspaper Der Neue Tag carried a detailed report in its 11th June edition, stating that:

> *"The entire adult male population was executed by firing squads. Women were*

*deported to concentration camps, and
children were sent to proper places for
their further upbringing. All buildings in
this village were levelled to the ground
and the name of the village was done
away with*".

The destruction had been filmed by Franz Treml, an advisor on photography to the local Nazi party. The film was shown throughout German-occupied territories, in an effort to discourage any further assassination attempts. The Nazis made it clear that Hitler's order was to be carried out quite literally. It wasn't enough to kill the occupants and destroy the buildings. They intended to erase all memory of Lidice.

The rest of the world reacted strongly to the Lidice massacre, which gave the Nazis pause when it came to the children. Nonetheless, in late June, Adolf Eichmann ordered their deaths. On 2nd July the remaining children were transported to the execution camp at Chełmno. Most of them died in the gas chambers there.

Around 340 people from Lidice were killed in the Nazi reprisals (192 men, 60 women, and 88 children). After the war,

153 women and 17 children returned. In total, it is estimated that 1,300 people were killed across Czechoslovakia in reprisals for Heydrich's death.

Death of Gabčík and Kubiš

Gabčík and Kubiš had given little thought to what they would do after their attack on Heydrich. Initially, they hid in safe houses, but the massive and sudden police searches made this difficult. The rapid, brutal reaction to Heydrich's death was making things difficult for them and everyone else involved in the resistance. A resistance man named Zelenka had contacts with the Greek Orthodox Karel Boromejsky church, which had a history of helping Czech nationalists. The lay preacher secured his bishop's permission to hide Gabčík, Kubiš, and five others. Church officials were sworn to secrecy and the men were hidden in the crypt, arriving one or two at a time.

Gabčík and Kubiš received the news of Heydrich's death while they were in the church. Their relief at the success of their mission quickly turned to horror as they learned of the innocent countrymen being killed in reprisals. The destruction of Lidice in particular weighed heavily on their minds. They considered sacrificing themselves, possibly committing suicide in public with placards around their necks stating that they had killed Heydrich.

Bishop Gorazd had originally given permission for the men to hide in the church. Now he decided that they were too big a risk, and wanted them moved. The resistance tried to find other places for the men to hide, ideally outside Prague. The scale of the German reprisals meant that few were willing to help. With nowhere to go, the men were trapped in the church.

Karel Čurda had parachuted into the protectorate from Britain as part of an operation codenamed Out Distance. He had been in Prague, but when the police started their huge search, he left to hide in his mother's barn at Nová Hlína in southern Bohemia. The sense of guilt around the reprisals against innocent Czechs wore him down. Eventually, he wrote an anonymous letter to the Czech police, in which he identified Gabčík and Kubiš as Heydrich's assassins. This did not appear to have any effect, so he took a train to Prague and walked into the Gestapo headquarters at Petschek Palace. There, he revealed the names of everyone he knew that had helped the assassins. The next day, the Gestapo raided the apartments of those named by Čurda. Under interrogation, those arrested revealed that Heydrich's assassins were in the church.

At 03:45 on 18th June, over 700 soldiers arrived at the church. Within half an hour, the church and the area around it was surrounded. Once the church was cut off, the Germans attacked. The battle lasted two hours. Kubiš and two other men were killed in the prayer loft. Eventually the Germans brought in fire engines to flood the crypt. The remaining four men, including Gabčík, committed suicide once it became clear that their position was hopeless.

Bishop Gorazd was arrested on 27th June. He tried to take all of the responsibility for sheltering the men. On

3rd September he was sentenced to death, along with the priests and lay leaders of the church. They were shot the next day. The Orthodox Church within the protectorate was dissolved, and its property confiscated.

Ležáky

Čurda's testimony led the Germans to the Pardubice region, where a group belonging to Operation Silver were active. The Gestapo found an illegal transmitter in the hamlet of Ležáky, and began making arrests in the area on 20th June. Alfréd Bartoš, one of the leaders of Operation Silver, was arrested on 21st June. He died from his wounds the next day.

At 12:30 on 24th June, Ležáky was surrounded by a combined force of the SS and protectorate police. The inhabitants were taken to Pardubice. All the houses in the hamlet were looted and burned. Of the 13 children, 11 were sent to the camp at Łódź and thence to Chełmno, where they were killed in a gas chamber. The remaining two, Jarmila and Marie Šťulík, were selected for Germanisation, but returned to Czechoslovakia after the war. All 33 of the adults were shot at nearby Pardubice Château.

Like Lidice, the events at Ležáky were announced publicly, on 26th June. Between October and December 1943, the ruins of the houses were pulled down and the ground levelled. Like Lidice, no trace of the little hamlet was left.

International Reaction

Some officials from the Czech government-in-exile suggested that the British government should retaliate. In particular, they wanted an announcement to the effect that, every time the Germans destroyed a village like Lidice, the RAF would destroy a German village or town with bombing raids. The issue was considered by the British War Cabinet on 15th June, less than a week after the destruction of Lidice. The suggestion would have been dangerous and difficult in practice, requiring many aircraft and a clear moonlit night. The War Cabinet decided that the forces would be better employed against "objectives of greater importance". The idea was rejected.

The atrocities committed across Czechoslovakia in the wake of Heydrich's death prompted the British foreign secretary, Anthony Eden, to send a message to the Czech foreign minister, Jan Masaryk, on 5th August. This message stated that Britain revoked the Munich Agreement. On 29th September 1942, the French National Assembly proclaimed that it considered the Munich Agreement null and void. By annulling the agreement, Britain and France promised to return the Sudetan territories to Czechoslovakia once the war against Germany was won.

This was very good news for the Czechs. The September 1938 Munich Agreement had ceded the Sudetenland area of Czechoslovakia to Germany. The agreement had been signed by Great Britain, France, Germany, and Italy. Notably, Czechoslovakia was not represented. The Czech government-in-exile had agitated constantly for the Allies to revoke the Munich agreement.

Lidice had been destroyed to demonstrate the Nazis' strength and the folly of opposing Hitler's will. The result was not what the Nazis expected. Instead of cowing the Allies, it served to increase their resolve. Even after years of war, people across the world were shocked at the sheer brutality meted out to the people of Lidice. In response, they made sure that Lidice would not be forgotten.

In the United States of America, the neighbourhood of Crest Hill in Chicago, Illinois was renamed to Lidice. In Pittsburgh, Pennsylvania, funds were raised for an ambulance aircraft that was named Spirit of Lidice. This aircraft served throughout the war, and afterwards helped to rebuild communities in war-damaged Europe. In Phillips, Wisconsin, a temporary memorial was unveiled in July 1943. The permanent and much more substantial monument was officially unveiled and dedicated at a ceremony on 27th August 1944. Both monuments were designed by Vaclav Hajny, a local Czech immigrant and coal miner's son. The small town of Tabor in South Dakota renamed a street to Lidice Street.

Towns in Mexico, Venezuela, Panama, and Brazil were renamed to Lidice, or incorporated Lidice into their names. San Jerónimo in Mexico was renamed San Jerónimo Lídice. The massacre is commemorated there every year on 10th June. Areas or streets in the cities of Coventry (UK) and Santiago (Chile) were renamed to commemorate the massacre. Parents of new-born baby girls chose to name them Lidice.

In 1942, a book-length verse play named The Murder of Lidice, by the American poet Edna St. Vincent Millay, was printed in Life magazine and published as a book. In 1943, it formed the basis of the film Hitler's Madman, directed by German-born Douglas Sirk. Another film about Lidice, The Silent Village, was released in the UK in the same year, and Czech composer Bohuslav Martinů composed an orchestral work entitled Memorial to Lidice.

The Lidice Shall Live Campaign

Dr Barnett Stross was a family doctor and city councillor in the British city of Stoke-on-Trent. He worked closely with the local miners and had done a great deal to improve their working conditions. When he heard of Lidice and Hitler's declaration that "Lidice shall die forever", his immediate response was "No. Lidice shall live". To this end, he decided to raise funds to pay for the reconstruction of Lidice.

At the conference of the Mineworkers' Federation of Great Britain in Blackpool in July 1942, Alderman Jones of Warwickshire raised the issue of Lidice. He suggested that the miners of Britain and the rest of the world should join together to raise funds. These funds would pay for a new village to be built on the site of the original Lidice.

The Lidice Shall Live campaign was officially launched on 6th September 1942. It was co-founded by Stross and Arthur Baddeley, the president of the North Staffordshire Miners' Federation. The Lord Mayor of Stoke-on-Trent was the committee president. The launch event was attended by 3,000 people, including Czech President Dr Edvard Beneš. Addressing the meeting, Beneš spoke of "the justice which we hope to achieve after the war". The president of the Miners' Federation of Great Britain, Will Lawther, and Aleksandr Bogomolov, the Soviet ambassador to the Polish government-in-exile, also attended.

When the campaign was launched, the tide of the war had started to turn in the Allies' favour, but the final outcome was still uncertain. The Dieppe raid in August had ended in disaster, with around 60% casualties. It was now obvious that an invasion of France would not be feasible for some time. In Britain, most food was rationed, a consequence of the U-boat campaign against merchant ships in the Atlantic Ocean. In the first six months of 1942, the Allies had lost over 500 ships, totalling over three million tons. In North Africa, a German attack had been stopped at the Battle of Alam el Halfa in August, but the Allies had yet to go on the offensive. In the Pacific, the Japanese had

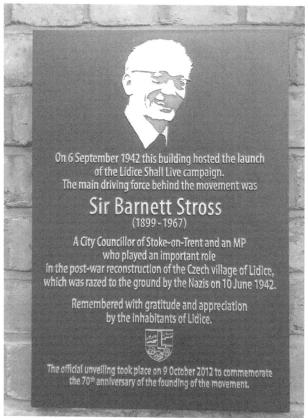

On 6 September 1942 this building hosted the launch
of the Lidice Shall Live campaign.
The main driving force behind the movement was

Sir Barnett Stross
(1899 - 1967)

A City Councillor of Stoke-on-Trent and an MP
who played an important role
in the post-war reconstruction of the Czech village of Lidice,
which was razed to the ground by the Nazis on 10 June 1942.

Remembered with gratitude and appreciation
by the inhabitants of Lidice.

The official unveiling took place on 9 October 2012 to commemorate
the 70th anniversary of the founding of the movement.

Plaque at the Regent Theatre

suffered a major defeat at the Battle of
Midway in June, but they still held most of
the territories they had gained in the
earlier part of the war.

Like Lidice, many towns and villages
around Stoke-on-Trent and the wider North

Staffordshire area were mining communities. Miners the world over share a bond forged by working in difficult and dangerous working conditions. As recently as New Year's Day 1942, mere months before the atrocity at Lidice, an explosion at Sneyd Colliery in Stoke-on-Trent had killed 56 men and injured many more. The closely knit community of Sneyd had been devastated by the loss. That tragedy must have been on the minds of many local miners when they heard of the atrocity perpetrated at Lidice.

Miners from Stoke-on-Trent and North Staffordshire pledged to give a day's wage each week to the Lidice Shall Live fund. By the end of the war, they had raised £32,000 (the equivalent of over £1,000,000 in 2016). Dr Stross worked tirelessly to organise further fund-raising campaigns across Britain, and many donations were received from abroad.

After the War

The re-instated Czech government's ministry of the interior launched a search for the children of Lidice. A list of names and ages was widely distributed, with photographs where available. The circular also asked for a search to be made for anyone involved in the kidnapping of the children. It described such people as "war criminals of a high measure of guilt". Help was requested from Allied and other countries to find the children. The Czech government made it clear that they wanted to both reunite the children with their mothers and punish those responsible.

Lina, Heydrich's wife, ended the war in the British zone of occupation. A Czech attempt to extradite her failed. She was tried in absentia and sentenced to life imprisonment. Karel Čurda had been paid five million crowns for the information that led the Germans to Heydrich's assassins. He was arrested by the resistance on 5th May 1945. Showing no remorse, he was tried by a revolutionary tribunal and executed.

Karl Herman Frank, Heydrich's deputy and the man who had orchestrated the reprisals, was tried at the People's Court in Prague during March and April 1946. Following his conviction for war crimes, he was sentenced to death. Five thousand spectators viewed his hanging on 22nd May 1946 at Pankrác prison in Prague. His body was buried in an anonymous pit at Ďáblice cemetery in Prague.

In June 1945, during a commemoration service and unveiling of a memorial, it was announced that a new village of Lidice was to be built. The Czech government planned to build the new village on the site of the old one. This was changed at the request of the survivors. The new village was built a few hundred metres from the original. The original site remained as a memorial to the dead. The money raised by the Lidice Shall Live campaign helped to pay for the new village, building of which began in 1947. A British delegation, headed by Will Lawther, the president of the Mineworkers Union, was present for the laying of the foundation stone.

The first part of the village was completed in 1949. The surviving women and children returned. The only men to survive were Horak and Stříbrný, who had served in the RAF during the war and whom the Gestapo had initially thought responsible for the assassination. The communist Czech government refused to allow them to return, and they stayed in the UK. The pear tree sapling that survived the destruction of the village grew into a full tree. It still survives, and is protected by the Czech government.

Dr Barnett Stross was awarded the Order of the White Lion, Czechoslovakia's highest decoration, in 1947. He visited Lidice several times, and a street in the new village was named after him. In 1957 he was awarded the freedom of Lidice. In the UK, he was awarded a knighthood for "political and public services" in the 1964 New Year's Honours list.

In 1954, a "Friendship and Peace Rose Garden" was created. This was based on plans by Stross, who organised a collection of 23,000 roses from 32 countries. The mass grave of the massacred men is marked by a cross with a crown of thorns. A memorial area with a museum and exhibition hall overlooks the site of the old village. An avenue of linden trees provides a link to the new village. In 1995, work began on a new memorial to the dead children of Lidice, by Marie Uchytilová. This memorial, completed in 2000, consists of 82 bronze statues of children, overlooking the site of the old village.

The hamlet of Ležáky was not rebuilt. A memorial was placed at the site of each destroyed building, commemorating the family that lived there. In 1966 a small museum and restaurant were built nearby.

In 1948, the Czech village of Beys was renamed Gabčíkovo in honour of Jozef

The children's memorial

Gabčík. When Czechoslovakia split on 1st January 1993, it became part of Slovakia. In 2016 a bust of Gabčík was erected in his home town of Poluvsie in northern Slovakia. It has been sited so that it looks on his childhood home. During a reorganisation in 1995, the Slovak 5th Special Forces Regiment Jozef Gabčík was created. It is the Slovak army's primary counter-terrorism and special operations unit.

Rebuilding Links with Stoke-on-Trent

In February 1948, a communist government was formed in Czechoslovakia. This concerned the West, which saw it as Soviet expansion in Europe. The Cold War was just beginning. Old allies were becoming enemies. Any link to communist countries became frowned upon, even considered treacherous by some. Dr Barnett Stross was elected MP for Stoke-on-Trent Central in 1950. He maintained close links with Lidice, but these links were increasingly viewed with suspicion. The tensions of the Cold War meant that the people of North Staffordshire almost forgot Lidice and their forefathers' generosity. To their credit, the people of Czechoslovakia, and later the Czech Republic, especially those of Lidice, never forgot how much the miners of North Staffordshire had given.

In May 2010 Alan and Cheryl Gerrard read of the Lidice Shall Live campaign in the Rupert Butler book, "An Illustrated History of The Gestapo". The couple immediately started working on restoring links between the communities and spreading awareness of Sir Barnett Stross' work. They started giving presentations about the story to local school children, and continue to do so. Local and national press were contacted to raise awareness, and they set up a dialogue with civic leaders in Lidice itself. They also called for Stoke-on-Trent to be officially twinned with Lidice, which was approved later that year.

The couple began a process of contributing to the Lidice Gallery's International Children's Exhibition of Fine Arts, ensuring that every child in Stoke-on-Trent had the chance to demonstrably celebrate their pride in the Lidice Shall Live campaign. Whilst researching the life of Sir Barnett Stross, Alan was invited to contribute to and open an exhibition celebrating his life in November 2010. They have laid a wreath on the mass grave of the 173 men murdered at Horak's Farm at every commemorative event since then. They laid the wreath on behalf of the people of Stoke-on-Trent when there was no civic delegation from the city. Otherwise, it was laid on behalf of the Friends of Barnett Stross. They continue to work to spread awareness of the story, and have helped many projects by other agencies.

Representatives of Stoke-on-Trent, Lidice, and the Lidice Memorial signed a memorandum of understanding in 2012. In the memorandum, they promised to inform and educate their local communities about the special link between the two towns, commemorate important anniversaries of the Lidice tragedy and the Lidice Shall Live campaign, and maintain exchange visits to help strengthen the bonds between them. In 2013, part of John Street in Stoke-on-Trent was renamed Lidice Way.

In 2013, the Stoke-on-Trent city council commissioned the Unearthed project, which had two aims: create a sculpture that would commemorate the tragedy of Lidice and remember the generosity of the local miners, as well as spread knowledge of the story. People were asked to make a promise to share the story with two other people. A tag, modelled on

The Unearthed sculpture

those worn by miners in 1942, was made for each promise. These tags would form a part of the sculpture. A series of events were held in the city to inform people of the story and collect promises. Later, around 300 promises were gathered from the residents of Lidice.

On 26th October 2013, the sculpture was unveiled, at a ceremony attended by the mayor of Stoke-on-Trent and a representative of the village of Lidice. The final sculpture stands 6.8 metres tall and has around 3,000 tags. In 1942, every miner had an individual tag. To identify its owner, the tag had the miner's initials and the first part of his date of birth. The tags on the sculpture use the same scheme to identify those who promised to spread the story of Lidice and the miners who helped rebuild it.

Web Resources

An interactive map, showing locations mentioned in this book, as well as other relevant locations, can be found at www.rpbook.co.uk/LidiceMap

A collection of videos related to the story can be found at www.rpbook.co.uk/LidiceVideos

Both will be updated if new information becomes available. If you have suggestions for either of them, please email me at russell@rpbook.co.uk

Digital Reinforcements: Free Ebook

To get a free ebook of this title, simply go to www.shilka.co.uk/dr and enter code LWFL96.

The free ebook can be downloaded in several formats: Mobi (for Kindle devices & apps), ePub (for other ereaders & ereader apps), and PDF (for reading on a computer). Ereader apps are available for all computers, tablets and smartphones.

About Russell Phillips

Russell Phillips writes books and articles about military technology and history. His articles have been published in Miniature Wargames, Wargames Illustrated, and the Society of Twentieth Century Wargamers' Journal. Some of these articles are available on his website. He has also been interviewed for the American edition of The Voice of Russia.

To get a free book and advance notice of new books, join Russell's mailing list at www.rpbook.co.uk/list. You can leave at any time.

Word of mouth is crucial for any author to succeed. If you enjoyed this book, please consider leaving a review where you bought it, or on a site like Goodreads. Even a short review would be very much appreciated.

Also by Russell Phillips

Operation Nimrod: The Iranian Embassy Siege

Red Steel: Soviet Tanks and Combat Vehicles of the Cold War

A Fleet in Being: Austro-Hungarian Warships of WW1

A Damn Close-Run Thing: A Brief History of the Falklands Conflict

This We'll Defend: The Weapons & Equipment of the U.S. Army

The Bear Marches West: 12 Scenarios for 1980s NATO vs Warsaw Pact Wargames

Find Russell Phillips Online

Website: www.rpbook.co.uk

Twitter: @RPBook

Google Plus: +RussellPhillips

Facebook: RussellPhillipsBooks

Goodreads: goodreads.com/RussellPhillips

E-mail: russell@rpbook.co.uk

Join Russell's mailing list: rpbook.co.uk/list

The Friends of Barnett Stross

Sir Barnett Stross (1899 - 1967) was leader of the Lidice Shall Live campaign, a genuine human rights campaigner at all levels, and a Save the Children co-founder. He was born on Christmas Day 1899 in Pabianice in the Vovoidship of Lodz, Poland.

The non-profit-making organisation The Friends of Barnett Stross works to raise awareness of Stross's work, of the Lidice atrocity of 1942, and of the role ordinary people around the world played in rebuilding the symbolic Czech village. The foundation encourages the development and exploration of cultural, economic, social, and educational links between the

UK, Czech Republic, and the wider international community.

At the time of writing, the organisation is cooperating with the Lidice Memorial on two projects highlighting the creative input which delivered the "new Lidice": a dilapidated house restored into a permanent exhibition space containing period features, which tells the story of the concept, design, and rebuilding of the new village; and secondly, a publication celebrating the Garden of Peace and Friendship. Both projects contain an emphasis on Sir Barnett Stross and send a message of love overcoming hate. Both will be launched at the 75th anniversary commemorative event in 2017.

Website: www.friendsofbarnettstross.org

C000112340

1 MONTH OF
FREE
READING

at
www.ForgottenBooks.com

By purchasing this book you are eligible for one month membership to ForgottenBooks.com, giving you unlimited access to our entire collection of over 1,000,000 titles via our web site and mobile apps.

To claim your free month visit:
www.forgottenbooks.com/free557783

ISBN 978-0-332-50903-7
PIBN 10557783

TOWN OF GILMANTON.

ANNUAL REPORT

OF THE

TOWN OFFICERS

FOR THE

YEAR ENDING FEBRUARY FIFTEENTH,
1901.

ANNUAL REPORTS

OF

TOWN OFFICERS

OF THE

TOWN of GILMANTON

COMPRISING THOSE OF THE

SELECTMEN, COLLECTOR, TREASURER, AUDITORS, TOWN CLERK AND SCHOOL BOARD.

FOR THE

FISCAL YEAR ENDING FEB. 15, 1901.

LACONIA, N. H.:

PRESS OF THE NEWS AND CRITIC.

1901.

TOWN OFFICERS.

SELECTMEN.

FRANK N. MERRILL.　　　　GEORGE E. PAGE,

STEPHEN L. WEEKS.

TOWN CLERK.

ROY C. EDGERLY.

TREASURER.

CHARLES H. GOODWIN.

COLLECTOR OF TAXES.

ERNEST H. GOODWIN.

AUDITORS.

GEORGE C. PARSONS.　　　HERBERT J. MARSH.

SUPERVISORS.

USHER S. PARSONS.　　　　LAUREL A. BLAKE.

DANIEL H. MOULTON.

SCHOOL BOARD.

LAURA E. VARNEY.　　　FRANK N. MERRILL.

C. FRANK PAGE.

BOARD OF HEALTH.

GEORGE H. BROWN.　　　　HARLAN PAGE,

GEORGE F. KELLEY.

POLICE.

FRANK G. OSBORNE.　　　SAMUEL E. EVELETH.

CONSTABLE.

CLARENCE N. COGSWELL.

FISH AND GAME WARDEN.

FRANK D. YOUNG.

Valuation and Taxation for 1900.

Real estate $362,122.00
Number of polls taxed, 306 . . . .   30,600.00
Horses, 414   · · 17,422.00
Oxen, 68 . . . .   3,550.00
Cows, 783 . . . .   18,446.00
Other neat stock, 471 . . . .   8,826.00
Sheep, 522 . . . .   1,412.00
Carriages, 2 . . . .   100.00
Stock in banks 4,300.00
Money on hand and at interest 3,316.00
Stock in trade 16,692.00
Mills and their machinery 9,732.00

                                                  $476,518.00
Amount of taxes levied for all purposes $9,387.40
        Rate of taxation $1.97 on $100.00.

COLLECTOR'S REPORT.

To the Taxpayers of the Town of Gilmanton:

I herewith submit my report as Collector:

Whole amount committed to me for collection . . .	$9,387.40
Whole amount collected and paid treasurer	9,387.40
I have received in abatements	60.03
In above abatements there was for over-tax and loss on animals and loss of buildings by fire	49.79
Actual abatements	10.24

I have collected interest of the following-named persons:

Horace T. Gilman . .	$0.02	Anna Edgerly	$0.04
Charles T. Smith . . .	.03	Herbert Sargent . . .	.04
Mary Woodman heirs .	.02	Walter J. Edgerly . . .	.03
Jasper R. Mudgett . .	.03	Charles D. Thyng .	.06
William N. Swain estate	.01	Sidney W. Linscott . .	.09
C. W. J. Peaslee estate .	.03	William Evans & C. . .	.01
Martha W. Moore . .	.02	Henry W. Dudley . .	.02
Euraldo P. Ellsworth .	.04	Walter H. Page . . .	.05
Aldis J. Lamprey . . .	.03	Lucy T. Page estate .	.10
Charles L. Chase . . .	.09	Alvin Prescott	.14
Calvin Jenkins	.02	Elmer J. Lord . . .	.23
George W. Nutter . .	.02	Mary L. Copp	.02
John W. Rollins . . .	.03	Jonathan Young estate .	.18
Lorrain Clough . . .	.02	John W. Sweatt . . .	.02
Ellsworth H. Rollins .	.02	J. D. & E. F. Nelson .	.38
Mary Gilman	.04	Lewis L. Towle . .	.02
Chas. A. Hilliard . . .	.04	Edwin J. Page	.07
John L. Clifford . . .	.03	Reuben Giles estate .	.05
Geo. W. Dow 2nd . . .	.06	Daniel Maxfield . . .	.01
Chauncey D. Gay . . .	.18	James D. Pease . . .	.04
Erling L. Gay	.01	Charlotte E. Weeks . .	.03
Henry S. Page	.15	John J. Smith	.05

Edward E. Smith . . .	.03	Ruel H. Hoadley . . .	.16
John P. Hussey . . .	.33	Henry C. Jones . . .	.01
Nancy K. Greenough .	.05	Nellie E. Zanes . . .	.02
Edwin J. Page	.06	Jeremiah W. Sanborn .	1.69
Chas. A. Dockham . .	.30	Ellen S. Pease	.02
Joel Sibly	.02	Albert H. Carr . . .	.01
John H. Haines . . .	.03	Laura Swain	.01
Chas. H. Chamberlain .	.05	Thomas Evans	.04
Ezekiel E. Witham . .	.05	Ezekiel A. Collins . .	.07
Amos R. Price	.06	Frank H. Sargent . .	.17
Warren M. Smith . . .	.03	Chas. E. Wilson . . .	.19
Ella A. Smith	.01	Harry W. Sanborn . .	.03
Ida L. Gault	.03	Leon Clement	.04
Sarah J. Twombly . .	.08	John S. Osborn estate .	.26
David Sawyer	.01	William P. Ashcroft . .	.13
Harriet S. Bond . .	.12	Herbert A. Twombly .	.04
Arabella Z. Knowles .	.06	Fred E. Rowe	.03
Daniel Dow	.05	Susan Batchelder . . .	.09
Charles W. Beck . . .	.03	Leander Hilliard . . .	.23
Richard Colcord . . .	.01	Joseph A. Spear . . .	.04
Chas. J. Hoadley . . .	.01	Smith C. Beck	.02
Lumian D. Marston .	.08	Geo. T. Worthington est.	.01
Martha J. Beck . . .	.11	Mary E. Haines estate .	.04
James H. Beck . .	.01	Belknap Savings Bank .	.44
Elwood H. Hill . .	.19	Morrill S. Jones . . .	.04
W. S. P. Sanderson . .	.22	Jessie F. Place	19
Frank M. Twombly . .	.07	F. A. Brown	.03
Ervil L. Smith	.21	Lorrain Durrell . . .	.42
Ernest C. Smith . .	.01	James H. Weeks . . .	1.05
Walter J. Edgerly . . .	.20		

Property sold for taxes 8.35

$19.01

ERNEST H. GOODWIN, Collector.

Gilmanton, N. H., February 15, 1901.

TREASURER'S REPORT.

CHARLES H. GOODWIN, Treasurer in Account with the Town of Gilmanton:

RECEIPTS.

1900.

Feb.	15.	To cash in hands of Treasurer . . .	$2,603.98
Apr.	28.	Received of selectmen money returned by highway surveyors of 1899 . . .	6.65
May	26.	Belknap County	306.35
June	30.	Selectmen	525.00
July	21.	Roy C. Edgerly, dog license in part .	90.00
Aug.	25.	Selectmen	200.00
	25.	Belknap County	238.67
	28.	Selectmen	300.00
Oct.	22.	Belknap County	64.75
Dec.	29.	Roy C. Edgerly, bal, dog license in full	48.24
	29.	Belknap County	245.72

1901.

Jan.	11.	State for railroad tax	4.38
	11.	State savings bank tax	1,091.28
	11.	State literary fund	110.50
	26.	Belknap County	55.00
Feb.	15.	E. C. Eastman, mortgage book returned	7.50
	15.	Ernest H. Goodwin, Collector . . .	9,387.40
	15.	" " int'rest	19.01

$15,304.43

EXPENDITURES.

PAID OUTSTANDING ORDERS AND INTERESTS.

1900.

Feb. 24. Congregational society Gilmanton Iron Works for interest on parsonage fuud for the year 1898 . . . . $ 5.12

Mar. 31. Cong. Society Gilmanton for interest on parsonage, for the year 1899 . . . . 5.15

31. Friends society Gilmanton for interest on parsonage fund for the year 1899 . 1.41

Ápr. 28. John Watson order No. 28, and interest in full 31.98

May 30. Trustees of Highland lodge, I. O. O. F., order No. 142, and interest in full . . 85.83

June 5. Ann P. Shannon, one year's interest on order No. 5, dated March 7, 1885 . . 5.15

5. Thos. Cogswell executor Jona. Young estate, order No. 91, and interest in full 257.29

21. Mary B. Cook, one year's interest on order No. 93, dated June 21, 1899 . . 12.00

21. Bertha L. Cook, one year's interest on order No. 94, dated June 21, 1899 . . 3.00

21. J. H. Nutter, one year's interest on order No. 95, dated June 21, 1899, drawn to J. H. Cook 2.55

29. Geo. E. Page, order in part 25.00

30. Ann P. Shannon, order and int. in full . 173.35

30. Laura F. Edgerly, one year's interest on order No. 20, dated March 14, 1896 . 5.10

30. Anna M. Hurd, one year's interest on order No. 50, dated March 28, 1885 . 2.80

30. Anna M. Hurd, one year's interest on order No. 103, dated June 23, 1899 . 1.20

Aug. 14.   Herbert N. Weeks for Laurenia A Eastman, one year's interest on order No.
63, dated July 23, 1889, drawn to Sarah
M. Gale $10.50

14.   Herbert N. Weeks, for Laurenia A. Eastman, one year's interest on order No.
50, dated June 26, 1889, drawn to
Sarah M. Gale 14.10

23.   Joseph A. Davis for Susan F. Davis, order
No. 104, dated June 12, 1899, drawn to
Jane Pendergast, principal and interest
in full 165.74

Oct. 23.   Edwin K. Jenkins, one year's interest on
order No. 195, dated Sept. 9, 1899 .   6.00

23.   Edwin K. Jenkins, order in part 125.00

Nov. 12.   John Watson, order and interest in full   162.34

29.   Nehemiah Durgin, one year's interest on
order No. 202, dated Oct. 28, 1899 .   15.00

Dec. 4.   Ernest H. Goodwin, one year's interest
on order No. 260, dated Dec. 4, 1899 .   33.00

27.   Laurenia A. Eastman, Admr'x, order No.
50, dated June 26, 1889, drawn to
Sarah M. Gale, principal and int. in full   477.08

27.   Laurenia A. Eastman, Admr'x, order No.
63, dated July 23,1889, drawn to Sarah
M. Gale, principal and interest in full   354.54

27.   Edwin K. Jenkins's order interest in full   75.50

29.   Melinda B. Avery, interest on order No.
25, dated April 14, 1888 to Jan. 1, 1901   13.71

29.   M. M. Lougee, interest on order No. 31,
dated March 25, 1881, to Jan. 1, 1901   4.12

Dec. 29.   Mary A. Nelson, interest on order No.
135, dated June 8, 1899 to Jan. 1, 1901   4.65

29.   Edwin S. Nelson, interest on order No.
134, dated June 8, 1899 to Jan. 1, 1901   9.30

29.   Mary Nelson, interest on order No. 71,
dated June 20, 1885 to Jan. 1, 1901 .   24.17

1901.

Jan.	4.	Natt H. Jones, order and interest in full .	$52.29
	9.	Sylvia Weeks, interest on order No. 154 dated July 20, 1899 to Jan. 1, 1901	4.34
	10.	Gertrude N. Kimball, interest on order No. 211, dated Oct. 28, 1899 to Jan. 1, 1901	10.57
	10.	Lucy A. Young, interest on order No. 210 dated Oct. 28, 1899 to Jan. 1, 1901 .	3.52
	10.	Hannah T. Edgerly, interest on order No. 253, dated June 24, 1899 to Jan. 1, 1901	4.55
	10.	Hannah T. Edgerly, interest on order No. 98, dated June 22, 1899 to Jan. 1, 1901	6.86
	10.	David G. Edgerly, interest on order No. 54, dated April 13, 1885 to Jan. 1, 1901	12.55
	10.	David G. Edgerly, interest on order No. 110, dated June 24, 1899 to Jan. 1, 1901	6.83
	16.	David G. Edgerly, interest on order No. 254, dated Nov. 25, 1899 to Jan. 1, 1901	16.50
	25.	Mary J. Potter, interest on order No. 86, dated June 20, 1899 to Jan. 1, 1901 .	2.29
	25.	Mary J. Potter, interest on order No. 173, dated Aug. 10, 1899 to Jan. 1, 1901 .	2.08
Jan.	26.	M. L. Dow, three years' interest on order No. 34, dated April 19, 1890	10.90
	31.	R. H. Frohock, order and interest in full	259.93
Feb.	1.	Cora B. Elkins, interest on order No. 147, dated July 22, 1899 to Jan. 1, 1901 .	2.15
	1.	Vona H. Page, interest on order No. 149, dated July 29, 1899 to Jan. 1, 1901 . .	2.13
	1.	Vona H. Page, two years' interest on order No. 96, dated Sept. 13, 1890, drawn to Vona Ham	6.00
	9.	George E. Page, interest on order No. 172 dated Aug. 26, 1899 to Jan. 1, 1901 .	2.16
	15.	Sarah A. Cotton, interest on order No. 92, dated June 20, 1899 to Jan. 1, 1901 .	16.07

Sarah A. Cotton, interest on order No. 183
dated Jan. 31, 1882 to Jan. 1, 1901 $8.45

$2,541.75

MISCELLANEOUS.

Charles A. Dockham, for mdse. and office
rent from Mar. 1, 1899 to Mar. 1, 1900 $31.31

Weeks Bros., for printing town reports
for year 1900 . . . .   42.50

George E. Shannon, for board of supervisors to Mar. 12, 1900 . . . . . .   1.50

Boston & Maine R R., for freight on
town reports, year 1900 40

Frank N. Merrill, for dinners furnished
town officers Mar. 13, 1900 . . . . .   2.25

Edwin J. Page, for travel and attendance
at supreme court, May 7, 1900 . . .   5.68

Thomas Cogswell, for rent of shoe factory,
March meeting, year 1900 . . . . .   10.00

Albert F. Page, for money appropriated
by the town for decorating soldiers'
graves, year 1900 . . . .   25.00

Charles E. Goodwin, for drawing drain
tiling from Alton 1.00

George C. Prescott, for use of watering
tub, for the year ending March 1, 1901   3.00

Edson C. Eastman, for highway summer
books, year 1900 . . . .   5.75

Weeks Bros., for printing tax bills, blanks
and other printed matter 5.50

Jay R. Munsey, for use of watering tub,
for the year ending Feb. 15, 1901 . .   3.00

A. A. Jones, for use of watering, tub for
the year ending Feb. 15, 1901 . . .   3.00

Nov.	24.	Sylvester Goodwin, for use of watering tub from Feb. 1900 to Feb. 1901 . .	$2.00
	24.	Madison C. Lamprey, for use of watering tub for the year ending Mar. 1, 1901 .	3.00
	24.	Mary L. Page, for dinners furnished town officers, town meeting day	2.40
Dec.	29.	Charles A. Dockham, for rent of office from Mar. 1, 1900 to Mar. 1, 1901 . .	30.00
	29.	Charles A. Dockham, for housing road machine two years	2.00
	29.	Alfred P. Ellsworth, for use of watering tub for the year ending Mar. 1, 1901 .	3.00
	29.	Charles A. Osborne, for use of watering tub for the year ending Mar. 1, 1901 .	3.00
	29.	Dr. Sullivan A. Taylor, for recording births and deaths	1.00
	20.	George E. Shannon, for board of supervisors, year 1900	1.25

1901.

Jan.	26.	School board express on books, year 1900	3.45
	26.	School board, for use telephone, stamps and use of checks, year 1900	2.75
	26.	F. N. Merrill, for use of telephone, Leavitt and Wilson cases, checks bought, stamps and stationery	4.47
	26.	F. N. Merrill, for copying 1900 invoice .	8.00
	26.	R. E Lane for printing return blanks .	1.00
Feb.	9.	James H. Weeks, for use of watering tub from Mar. 1, 1900 to Mar. 1, 1901 . .	3.00
	9.	Mary B. Cook, for use of watering tub from Mar. 1, 1900 to Mar. 1, 1901, . .	3.00
	15.	Frank N. Merrill, expenses and services of self and team in Leavitt, Wilson and Ransom cases	7.50
	15.	Weeks Bros., for printing tax bills and other matter for collector, year 1900 .	3.25

Feb. 15. Thomas Cogswell, for rent of shoe factory
fall election, year 1900 . . . . $10.00

15. Thomas Cogswell, in full services rendered, year ending Feb. 15, 1901. . .   56.00

15. Fisk A. Durrell, for use of watering tub
from Mar. 1, 1899 to Mar. 1, 1901 . .   4.00

15. George E. Shannon, for board of selectmen and horse baiting, year ending
Feb. 15, 1901 . . . .   11.75

15. Daniel Connell, for horse keeping for
selectmen and supervisors, year ending
Feb. 15, 1901 . . . .   4.70

15. Ernest H. Goodwin, for taxes, interest and
cost on the same assessed on property
sold the town year 1901 . . . . . .   384.97

———————

$695.38

ROADS AND BRIDGES.

1900.

Feb. 24. Owen J. Edgerly, labor on highway in 1899 $1.62

Jan. 27. Romie Little for labor on highway in 1899   1.87

Mar. 19. John F. Battis, for labor on highway,
year 1899 . . . .   7.61

31. Walter H. Ayer, labor on highway in 1899   6.00

June 2. Charles P. Sargent, for labor on highway
summer of 1900 as agent 36.00

2. John W. Brown, for labor on highway,
summer of 1900 as agent 36.00

2. Walter Ayer, for labor on highway, summer of 1900 as agent (in part) . . .   30.00

9. Riley M. Bickford, for labor on highway
summer of 1900 as agent 36.00

30. George C. Parsons, for labor on highway
summer agent, year 1900 . . . . .   60.00

30. Daniel Dow, for labor on highway as
summer highway agent 37.00

June	30.	Eugene L. Mudgett, for labor on highway as summer highway agent	$23.00
	30.	Stephen L. Weeks, for labor on highway as summer highway agent	40.00
	30.	Elbridge G. Clough, for labor on highway as summer highway agent . . .	90.00
	30.	Romie Little, for labor on highway as summer highway agent	17.50
	30.	Marcus S. Weeks, for labor on highway as summer highway agent	45.00
	30.	Stephen W. Sargent, for labor on highway as agent, summer 1900 . . .	60.00
	30.	Moses N. Downing, for labor on highway as summer highway agent . .	40.00
	30.	Stephen W. Sargent, for labor on Nelson bridge, year 1900	5.00
	30.	Fred S. Cotton, for labor on highway as summer highway agent	55.00
	30.	Fred V. Pease, for labor on highway as summer highway agent	45.00
	30.	Frank W. Foss, for labor on highway as summer highway agent	36.00
	30.	Charles F. Sargent, for labor on highway as summer highway agent	96.00
	30.	Frank R. Griffin, for labor on highway as summer highway agent	45.00
	30.	Charles H. Shannon, for labor repairing bridges	1.75
	30.	Henry E. Page, for labor on highway as summer highway agent	50.00
	30.	Usher S. Parsons, for labor on highway as summer highway agent	36.00
	30.	Walter S. Green, for labor on highway as summer highway agent	36.00
	30.	Charles M. Batchelder, labor on highway as summer agent	24.75

June 30. Edmund C. Varney, for labor on highway
          as summer highway agent $60.00

30. George E. Page, for labor on highway, as
     summer highway agent 40.00

30. Joseph L. Jones, for labor on highway as
     summer highway agent 20.00

30. Rufus A. Knowles, for labor on highway
     as summer highway agent 20.00

30. Stephen L. Weeks, for bridge plank fur-
     nished the R. A. Knowles' district . 19.84

30. J. Horace Beck, for labor on highway as
     summer highway agent 33.17

30. Merwin E. French, for labor on. highway
     as summer highway agent 45.00

July 21. Charles A. Price, for labor on highway as
          summer highway agent, 1900 . . . . 50.00

28 Irving A. Clough, for labor on highway
    as agent, 1900 . . .   . 40.00

28 Joseph L. Jones, for labor on highway as
    agent, 1900 . . . . 14.00

28 Charles D. Weare, for labor on highway
    as agent, 1900 . . . . 45.00

Aug. 2. George W. Dow 2nd, for labor on high-
          way as agent, 1900 . . . . 45.00

15 Frank M. Twombly, for labor on highway
    as agent, year 1900 . . . . 25.00

25 Elbridge G. Clough, for labor on highway
    as agent, 1900 . . . . 15.00

25 True F. Osborne, for labor on highway as
    highway agent, 1900 . . . . . . $45.00

25 True F. Osborne, for labor on highway as
    highway agent, 1900 . . . . 19.00

25 Usher S. Parsons, for labor on highway
    as agent, 1900 . . . . 14.00

Aug. 25. H. W. Downing, for labor on highway as
          agent, 1900 . . . . 24.00

Aug.	27.	L. W. Downing and son, for labor on highway in 1899	$2.86
	29.	Jeremiah S. Leavitt, for labor on highway, winter 1899	3.00
Sept.	15.	John C. Riley, for labor on highway as highway agent, 1900	24.00
	29.	John W. Ham, for labor on highway as highway agent, 1900	20.00
	29.	Elbridge G. Clough, for labor on highway as highway agent, 1900	20.00
	29.	Charles P. Sargent, for labor on highway as highway agent, year 1900	6.00
	29.	Stephen L. Weeks, for labor on highway as highway agent, summer 1900 . . .	5.00
Oct.	22.	Romie Little, for labor on highway as agent, summer 1900	17.50
	27.	Stephen W. Sargent, for labor and lumber for repairing Nelson bridge	8.89
	27.	The Downing Co., for drain pipe bought in 1900	23.31
Nov.	6.	Elbridge G. Clough, for labor on highway as highway agent, year 1900	26.00
	6.	Charles E Plummer, for labor on highway as summer highway agent, 1900 . . .	63.00
	24.	George E. Page, for labor on highway as agent, summer of 1900	3.94
	24.	Rufus A. Knowles, for labor on highway as agent, summer of 1900	25.00
	24.	Frank M. Twombly, for labor on highway, summer of 1900	13.00
	24.	C. M. Batchelder, for labor on highway, summer of 1900	11.25
	24	C. H. Stevens & Co., for bridge plank furnished town, year 1900	24.54
	24	Jay R. Munsey, for labor on highway, summer of 1900	5.00

Nov.	24	Stephen W. Sargent, for labor on high-way as agent, summer 1900	$3.13
Dec.	29.	John P. Hussey, for bridge plank labor on town hall and mouldboard fur-nished in 1900	36.86
	29	Jeremiah W. Sanborn, for labor on high-way as agent, summer 1900 . . .	47.11
	29	Aldis J. Lamprey, for labor on highway year 1900	6.00
	29	J. Horace Beck, for labor and lumber re-pairing Lucy bridge, year 1900 . . .	13.47
	29	E. J. Lord, for bridge plank furnished the town and damage to wheel	26.44
	29	Walter H. Ayer, for labor on highway as agent, summer 1900	12.00

1901.

Jan.	12.	William E. Smith, for labor on highway, summer of 1900	1.75
	26.	Merwin E. French, for labor, bridge plank and timber, furnished the town . .	7.12
	26.	Edmand C. Varney, for labor on highway as agent, summer of 1900	18.73
	26.	Edwin F. Nelson, for bridge plank fur-nished the town, 1159 feet	12.75
	26.	Elbridge G. Clough, for labor on highway as agent summer of 1900	8.00

$2,067.76

ABATEMENTS.

1900.

Mar.	19.	Mathes and Perley, for abatement for overtax in 1899	$2.35
Aug.	25.	Ernest H. Goodwin, abatement of overtax assess'd ag'inst Joseph Brake, year 1900	5.83
	25.	Ernest H. Goodwin, for abatement of overtax assessed against William Dear-born, year 1900	5.88

Aug. 25. Ernest H. Goodwin, for abatement of taxes assessed against William Moody, year 1900 . . . . $1.97

27. Frank N. Merrill, for abatement of taxes assessed in the year 1899 . . . . . 13.00

27. Frank N. Merrill, for abatement of over-tax assessed in the year 1899 . . . . 13.72

Sept. 29. George W. Munsey, for abatement of overtax on poll, year 1900 . . . . . 1.97

29. Charles P. Sargent, for abatement of overtax, year 1900 . . . . 3.94

29. Charles F. Merrill, for abatement on loss of buildings by fire 9.45

Nov. 6. Owen J. Edgerly, for abatement of poll taxes, 1896, '97, '98 and '99, overtax . 8.24

24. Ernest H. Goodwin, for abatement of overtax assessed against Willard G. McClary on poll, year 1900 . . . . 1.97

24. Ernest H. Goodwin, for abatement of overtax assessed against Jesse Ordway on poll, year 1900 . . . . 1.97

24. Ernest H. Goodwin, for abatement of poll tax assessed against John Bagley, year 1900 . . . . 1.97

24. Ernest H. Goodwin, for abatement of overtax on poll assessed against Oscar Ellsworth, year 1900 . . . . 1.97

24. Joseph Leyland, for abatement of over-tax, year 1900 49

24. Thomas B. Lane, for John H. Carr heirs, overtax, year 1900 . . . . 5.91

24. George W. Nutter, for abatement of taxes, loss of buildings by fire, overtax . . 4.53

28. Henry Buswell, for abatement of tax on horse lost, year 1900 . . . . 1.18

Dec. 29. John J. Smith, for abatement of overtax year 1900 . . . . 1.30

1901.

Jan. 26. Eugene O. Plummer, for abatement of
poll tax, year 1900, paid in Mass. . . $1.97

26. Leander A. Hilliard, for abatement of
poll tax, year 1899, paid in Canterbury   1.96

Feb. 15. Ernest H. Goodwin, for abatement of
Edwin Flander's poll tax paid in Alton
year 1900 . . . .   1.97

15. Ernest H. Goodwin, for abatement of
taxes assessed Jeremiah S. Leavitt,
year 1900 . . . .   4.33

15. Ernest H. Goodwin, for abatement of poll
tax assessed against Harry L. Brown
year 1900 . . . .   1.97

                                        ———————
                                        $99.79

COUNTY POOR.

Feb. 24. Caleb P. Webster, for aid to self from
· Jan. 24 to Feb. 21, 1900 . . . . . .   6.00

24. George E. Shannon, for aid to transients
to Feb. 15, 1900 . . . .   1.50

24. Henry Canney, for aid to transients to
Feb. 15, 1900 . . . .   ·4.50

24. Nancy K. Greenough, for aid to Melvin
and Addie Greenough from Jan. 23 to
Feb. 20, 1900 . . . .   12.00

24. S. K. Twombly, for aid to Addie Evans
and Blanche Adams from Jan. 27, to
Feb. 24, 1900 . . . .   12.00

Mar. 31. Samuel E. Eveleth one-half cord wood for
Richard R. Colcord 2.00

31. George E. Shannon, for aid to transients
to March 3, 1900 . . . .   3.75

31. John S. Morrison, for board furnished
Laura A. Page from Jan. 30 to April
3, 1900 . . . .   9.00

Mar.	31.	Nancy K. Greenough, for board furnished Greenough children from Feb. 20, to Mar. 27, 1900 and shoes and rubbers	16.65
	31.	John M. Connell, for aid furnished Henry L. Ransom from Jan. 27 to Apr. 1, 1900	8.10
	31.	John M. Connell, for aid furnished Fannie E. Gordon from Feb. 1 to Apr. 1, 1900	12.75
	31.	Caleb P. Webster, aid to self from Feb. 21 to Mar. 28, 1900	7.50
	31.	Jay R. Munsey, for aid to C. A. Twombly in the months of Feb. and Mar. 1900 .	4.03
	31.	Mrs. S. K. Twombly, for aid furnished to Adams' children from Feb. 24 to Mar. 31, 1900	15.00
	31.	George E Shannon, for aid furnished transients	1.00
Apr.	28.	John S. Morrison, for board of Laura A. Page from Apr. 3 to May 1, 1900 . .	4.00
	28.	Nancy K. Greenough, for board and shoes furnished Greenough children from Mar. 27 to Apr. 24, 1900 . . .	13.30
	28.	Mrs. S. K. Twombly, for boarding Blanche Adams and Addie Evans from Mar. 31 to Apr. 28, 1900	12.98
May	26.	Mrs. S. K. Twombly, for boarding Blanche Adams and Addie Evans from Apr. 28 to May 26, 1900	12.00
	26.	John M. Connell, for aid furnished Fannie E. Gordon from Apr. 1 to June 1, 1900	12.01
	26.	John M. Connell, for aid furnished Henry L. Ransom from Apr. 1 to June 1, 1900	7.21
	26.	Mrs. Nancy K. Greenough, for boarding Greenough children from Apr. 24 to May 22, 1900	12.00

May   26. John S. Morrison, for board of Laura A.
            Page from May 1 to May 29, 1900 . $4.00
June   3. George E. Shannon, for aid to transient   .75
   .   30. Mrs. Nancy K. Greenough, for board
            furnished Melvin and Addie Greenough
            . from May 22 to June 26, 1900 . . .   16.00
       30. Mrs. S. K. Twombly, for board of Addie
            Evans and Blanche Adams from May
            26 to June 30, 1900 . . . .   16.80
       30. John S. Morrison, for board of Laura A.
            Page from May 29 to July 3, 1900 . .   5.00
July   28. George W. Dow, 2d, for wood furnished
            Richard R. Colcord, year 1900 . . .   2.00
       28. Mrs. S. K. Twombly, for board furnished
            Addie Evans and Blanche Adams from
            June 30 to July 28, 1900 . . . . . .   12.00
       28. Nancy K. Greenough, for board and shoes
            furnished Greenough children from
            June 26 to July 24, 1900 . . . . . .   13.00
       28. John S. Morrison, for board of Laura A.
            Page from July 3 to July 31, 1900 . .   4.00
       28. John M. Connell, for aid furnished Fannie
            Gordon from June 1 to Aug. 1, 1900 .   13.59
       28. John M. Connell, for aid furnished Henry
            L. Ransom from June 1 to July 25, 1900   8.18
Aug.   25. Mrs. Nancy K. Greenough, for boarding
            the Greenough children from July 24 to
            Aug. 28, 1900 . . . .   15.00
       25. Mrs. S. K. Twombly, for boarding Addie
            Evans and Blanche Adams from July
            28 to Aug. 25, 1900 . . . .   12.00
       25. John S. Morrison, for aid furnished Laura
            A. Page from July 31 to Sept. 4, 1900 . 5.00
Sept. 29. Mrs. S. K. Twombly, for board and shoes
            furnished Blanche Adams and Addie
            Evans from Aug. 15 to Sept. 29, 1900 . 17.00

Sept. 29. Nancy K. Greenough for board and shoes furnished Greenough children from Aug. 28 to Sept. 24, 1900 . . . . . $13.00

29. John M. Connell, for aid furnished Fannie Gordon from Aug. to Oct. 1, 1900   13.59

29. John M. Connell, for aid furnished Henry L. Ransom from Aug. 1 to Oct. 1, 1900 . . . . 8.16

Oct. 27. Mrs. Nancy K. Greenough, boarding Greenough children and shoes furnished from Sept. 24 to Oct. 23, 1900   13.70

27. Mrs. S. K. Twombly, for boarding Addie Evans and Blanche Adams from Sept. 29 to Oct. 27, 1900 . . . . 12.00

27. R. H. Langley, for aid furnished R. R. Colcord March 24, 1900 . . . . . . 1.25

27. Harlan Page, member of board of health, for services and expenses rendered Harry Howard during sickness with typhoid fever 22.98

Nov. 24. Dudley N. Page, for boarding Laura A. Page from Sept. 4 to Nov. 27. 1900 .   12.00

24. Nancy K. Greenough, for boarding the Greenough children and shoes furnished from Oct. 23 to Nov. 20, 1900 . . . 13.70

24. Mrs. S. K. Twowbly, for boarding Addie Evans and Blanche Adams and shoes furnished from Oct. 27 to Nov. 24, 1900   13.00

24. John M. Connell, for supplies furnished Fannie Gordon from Oct. 1 to Nov. 19, 1900 . . . . 12.00

24. John M. Connell, for supplies furnished Henry L. Ransom from Oct. 1 to Nov. 19, 1900 . . . . 7.20

24. Dr. C. P. Ballard, for medical services rendered Harry Howard from Sept. 16 to Oct. 17, 1900 . . . . 27.00

Dec. 29. Nancy K. Greenough, for boarding Greenough children from Nov. 20 to Dec.
25, 1900 . . . . $15.00

29. George E. Shannon, for aid to transients   2.25

29. Mrs. S. K. Twombly, for boarding Addie
Evans and Blanche Adams from Nov.
24 to Dec. 29, 1900 . . . .   15.00

1901.

Jan. 26. Dudley N. Page, for boarding Laura A.
Page from Nov. 26, 1900 to Jan. 22,
1901 . . . .   9.00

26. John M. Connell, for supplies furnished
Fannie Gordon from Nov. 27, 1900 to
Feb. 1, 1901 . . . .   13.46

26. John M. Connell, for supplies furnished
H. L. Ransom from Dec. 8, 1900 to
Feb. 1, 1901 . . . .   8.11

26. Mrs. S. K. Twombly, for boarding Addie
Evans and Blanche Adams from Dec.
29, 1900 to Jan. 26, 1901 . . . . .   13.00

26. Nancy K. Greenough, for boarding Melvin and Alice Greenough and supplies
furnished from Dec. 25, 1900 to Jan.
22, 1901 . . . .   13.60

26. George E. Shannon, for aid to transients,
year 1900 . . . .   1.75

$594.35

AID TO DEPENDENT SOLDIERS.

1900.

June 2. The City Market, for aid furnished Sam'l
Swain from Feb. 1 to May 1, 1900 . . $30.55

Aug. 25. Lougee Bros., for clothing furnished Sam'l
Swain 9.50

25. Arthur C. Randlett, for aid furnished Sam'l
Swain from May 1 to Aug. 1, 1900 . .   33.25

Nov. 24. Arthur C.Randlett, for aid furnished Sam'l
Swain from Aug. 1 to Nov. 1, 1900 . . $32.69

1901.

Feb. 9. A. C. S. Randlett, for supplies furnished
Sam'l B. Swain from Nov. 1, 1900 to
Feb. 1, 1901 . . . .   33.64

                                        _____

                                        $139.63

DEPENDENT SOLDIERS CHARGEABLE TO COUNTY.

Feb. 24. Helen J. Bean, for aid to Mary J. Ryan
from Jan. 24 to Feb. 24, 1900 . . . . $10.00

24. Clara F. Bean, for house rent furnished
Mrs. D. F. Ryan from Nov. 19 to Feb.
19, 1900 . . . .   6.00

24. Mrs. L. W. Downing, for aid to Elizabeth
P. Morrill from Jan. 23 to Feb. 20, 1900   8.00

Mar. 31. Helen J. Bean, for aid to Mary J. Ryan
from Feb. 28 to Mar. 28, 1900 . . .   15.00

31. Mrs. L. W. Downing for board of Elizabeth P. Morrill from Feb. 20 to Mar.
27, 5 weeks 10.00

Apr. 28. Mrs. L. W. Downing, for board of Mrs.
Elizabeth P. Morrill from Mar. 27 to
April 24, 1900 . . . .   8.00

28. Helen J. Bean, for supplies furnished Mary
J. Ryan from Mar. 28 to Apr. 24, 1900   10.75

May 26. Mrs. L. W. Downing, for board of Mrs.
Elizabeth P. Morrill from April 24 to
May 22, 1900 . . . .   8.00

26. Helen J. Bean, for aid furnished Mrs.
Mary J. Ryan from May 1 to June
1, 1900 . . . .   8.75

26. Clara F. Bean, for house rent furnished
Mrs. Mary J. Ryan from Feb. 19 to
May 19, 1900 . . . .   6.00

June	30.	Helen J. Bean, for aid furnished Mrs. Mary J. Ryan from June 1 to July 1, 1900	$12.25·
	30.	Mrs L. W. Downing, for board of Mrs. Elizabeth P. Morrill from May 22 to June 26, 1900	10.00
July	28.	Mrs. L. W. Downing, for board furnished Mrs. Elizabeth P. Morrill from June 26 to July 24, 1900	8.00
Aug.	25.	Clara F. Bean, for aid furnished Mary J. Ryan from July 25 to Aug. 22, 1900 .	8.00
	25.	Clara F. Bean, for labor plowing garden for Mrs. Mary J. Ryan, spring 1900 .	1.00
	25	Clara F. Bean, for aid furnished Mary J. Ryan from July 1 to July 25, 1900 . .	10.00
	25.	Clara F. Bean, for house rent furnished Mary J. Ryan from May 19 to Aug. 19, 1900	6.00
	25.	Stephen L. Weeks, for 1½ cords of wood furnished Mary J. Ryan	3.00
	25.	Mrs. L. W. Downing, for boarding Mrs. Elizabeth P. Morrill from July 24, to Aug. 21, 1900	8.00
Sept.	29.	Mrs. L. W. Downing, for board furnished Mrs. Elizabeth P. Morrill from Aug. 21, to Sept. 25, 1900	18.00
	29.	Stephen L. Weeks, for one-half cord of wood furnished Mary J. Ryan . . .	3.00
Oct.	27.	Mrs. L. W. Downing, for boarding Elizabeth P. Morrill from Sept. 25 to Oct. 23, 1900	8.00
Nov.	3.	Clara F. Bean, for aid furnished Mrs. Mary J. Ryan from Aug. 1, to Oct. 1, 1900	10.00
	3.	Clara F. Bean, for aid furnished Mary J. Ryan from Oct. 1, to Nov. 1, 1900 . .	8.00

Nov. 24. Mrs. L. W. Downing, for boarding Elizabeth P. Morrill from Oct. 23 to Nov.
20, 1900 . . . . $8 00

24. Stephen L. Weeks, for 1½ cords of wood
furnished Mary J. Ryan in Nov. 1900 .   4.00

30. Clara F. Bean, for house rent for Mary J.
Ryan from Aug. 19 to Nov. 19, 1900 .   6.00

30. Clara F. Bean, for supplies furnished
Mary J. Ryan from Oct. 1, to Nov. 21,
1900 . . . .   8.00

Dec. 29. Clara F. Bean, for supplies furnished
Mary J. Ryan from Nov. 21, to Jan. 1,
1901 . . . .   10.00

29. Stephen L. Weeks, for 1½ cords of wood
furnished Mary J. Ryan in Nov. 1900   5.00

29. Mrs. L. W. Downing, for Mrs. Elizabeth
P. Morrill from Nov. 20 to Dec. 25,
1900, five weeks 10.00

1901

Jan. 26. Clara F. Bean, for supplies furnished
Mary J. Ryan from Jan. 1 to Feb.
1, 1901 . . . .   8.00

26. Lucia D. Blake, for aid to self from Jan.
1, to Jan. 28, four weeks 4.00

26. Mrs. L. W. Downing, for boarding Mrs.
Elizabeth P. Morrill from Dec. 25,
1900 to Jan. 25, 1901 . . . .   8.00

_____

$266.75

POOR OF TOWN.

1900.

Feb. 24. Helen J. Bean, for aid to Charles A. Hilliard from Jan. 23 to Feb. 20, 1900 . $4.00

24. R. H. Langley, for aid to Charles A. Hilliard from Aug. 18 to Sept. 4, 1899 .   1.03

24. R. H. Langley, for aid to Richard R. Colcord to Feb. 21, 1900 . . . .   2.75

Mar.	31.	Helen J. Bean, for aid furnished C. A. Hilliard from Feb. 26 to Mar. 26, 1900 .	$5.00
Apr.	28.	Mrs. A. W. Smith, for board of Mrs. Bean from Dec. 28, 1899 to April 26, 1900 .	38.25
	28.	Helen J. Bean for supplies furnished Charles A. Hilliard from Apr. 1 to Apr. 24, 1900	4.00
May	26.	Helen J. Bean, for aid furnished Charles A. Hilliard from Apr. 24 to May 25, 1900	3.90
June	30.	Helen J. Bean, for aid furnished C. A. Hilliard from June 1 to July 1, 1900 . .	5.00
	30.	Mrs. A. W. Smith, for board of Mrs. Bean from April 27, to June 28, 1900,	20.25
July	28.	George E. Page, for digging grave for William Moody	2.00
Aug.	25.	E. J. Lord, for burial outfit and services burying William Moody	20.00
	25.	Helen J. Bean, for aid furnished Charles A. Hilliard from May 29, to July 14, 1900	7.00
Sept.	29.	Mrs. A. W. Smith, for board of Mrs. W. Bean from June 28, to Sept. 27, 1900, thirteen weeks	29.25
Dec.	29.	Mrs. A. W. Smith, for board of Mrs. W. Bean from Sept 27, to Dec. 27, 1900,	29.25
	29.	Dr. Sullivan A. Taylor, for medical attendance rendered Mrs. Bean	1.10
1901.			
Jan.	26.	E. J. Lord, for use of team conveying Jeremiah Leavitt to county farm . .	3.00
Feb.	15	Frank N. Merrill, for services of self and team expenses in Will Moody case .	2.00
	15	Charles T. Smith, for aid to transient, year 1901	1.50

$179.28

TOWN OFFICERS.

Feb.	24.	Charles D. Weare, for services as selectman and board in full to Feb. 15, 1900	$27.00
	24.	Charles D. Weare, for services as selectman and board out of town to Feb. 15, 1900	9.50
	24.	Nehemiah Durgin, for services as selectman and board in full to Feb. 15, 1900	40.00
	24.	Herbert J. Marsh, for services as auditor for the year ending Feb. 15, 1900 . .	6.50
	24.	George C. Parsons, for services as auditor for the year ending Feb. 15, 1900	6.50
Mar.	31.	Nehemiah Durgin, for services as selectman from Feb. 15 to Mar. 13, 1900 .	11.75
May.	26.	Thomas Cogswell Jr., for services as town clerk from Feb. 15 to Mar. 13, 1900	6.00
	31.	C. D. Weare, for services as selectman and board and money paid out from Feb. 15 to Mar. 13, 1900	10.43
Aug.	27.	Frank N. Merrill, for services as tax collector, year 1899	100.00
Sept.	29.	John W. Ham, for services as selectman from Feb. 15 to Mar. 14, 1900 . . .	10.00
Nov.	24.	Frank G. Osborne, for services as constable from July 4, 1899 to Nov. 6, 1900	6.00
	24.	Usher S. Parsons, for services as supervisor of check list for the year 1900 .	14.00
	24.	L. A. Blake, for services as supervisor and horse baiting from Feb. 24 to Nov. 6, 1900	12.45
	24.	George E. Page, for services as selectman in part for the year 1900 . . .	38.93
Nov.	24.	Stephen L. Weeks, for services as selectman in part for the year 1900	35.00
Dec.	29.	Albert F. Page, for services as ballot inspector, year 1900	2.00

Dec. 29. R. F. Varney, for services as ballot in-
          spector, year 1900 . . . . $2.00

1901.

Jan. 26. Horace T. Gilman, for services as ballot
          inspector, year 1900 . . . .   2.00

     23. E. J. Lord, for services as ballot inspector,
          year 1900 . . . .   2.00

          Daniel H. Moulton, for services as supervisor,
          year 1900 . . . .   9.00

Feb. 9. Roy C. Edgerly, for services as town
          clerk, year 1900 . . . .   31.81

     15. Winfield S. Shannon, for services in full
          to Feb. 15, 1901, as clerk of school dis-
          trict 6.31

     15. Frank N. Merrill, in full for services as
          selectment, year ending Feb. 15, 1901,   58.00

     15. George E. Page, balance for services as
          selectmen, year ending Feb. 15, 1901,   12.25

     15. Stephen L. Weeks, in full for services
          and board for the year ending Feb. 15,
          1901 . . . .   21.00

     15. Ernest H. Goodwin, in full for services as
          tax collector for the year ending Feb.
          15, 1901 . . . .   100.00

     15. Chas. H. Goodwin, in full for services as
          town treasurer, year ending Feb. 15,
          1901 . . . .   60.00
                                                     ─────────
                                                      $640.43

SCHOOL MONEY.

1901.

Feb. 15. Treasurer of school board school money
          for the year 1900 . . . . $1,448.73

EXPENSES OF SCHOOL BOARD.

Aug. 27. Frank N. Merrill, for services as member
          of school board, year 1899 . . . . .   40.00

Feb. 15. Frank N. Merrill, for services as member
of school board, year ending Feb. 15,
1901 . . . . $30.00

15. C. Frank Page, for services as member of
school board, year ending Feb. 15, 1901   30.00

15. Laura E. Varney, for services as member
of school board, year ending Feb. 15,
1901 . . . .   30.00
_____
$130.00

SCHOOL SUPPLIES.

Oct. 22. American Book Co., for books furnished
schools, years 1899 and 1900 . . . . $125.00

Nov. 6. George F. Cram, for supplies furnished
schools 11.40

24. Thomas R. Sherwell & Co., for supplies,
books furnished schools, year 1900 .   30.75

24. Levenworth & Myer, for school supplies,
books furnished schools, year 1900 . .   15.95

24. Sibley & Tucker, for school supplies,
books furnished schools, year 1900 . .   5.50

1901.
Jan. 26. Thompson, Brown & Co., for books furnished schools, year 1900 . . . .   2.50
_____
$191.10

SCHOOL HOUSE REPAIRS.

1900.
Feb. 15. Treasurer of school board balance of order
No. 19, drawn Feb. 24, 1900, for school
house repairs, year 1900 . . . . . .   34.22

15. Treasurer of school board in full for
school house repairs 224.07
_____
$258.29

COUNTY TAX.

1900.

Aug. 25. County tax in part $350.00
Sept. 21.   "   " 643.56
Oct. 22.   "   " 300.00
Nov. 9. Balance of tax in full 200.00

$1,493.56

STATE TAX.

1901.

Jan. 9. Solan A. Carter, state treasurer, state
tax $986.00

TOWN LIBRARY,

1901.

Feb. 15. Library appropriation for 1900 . . . . $76.20

DAMAGE TO DOMESTIC ANIMALS,

1901.

Feb. 15. Clarence N. Cogswell, for services as dog
constable year ending Feb. 15, 1901 . $10.00
15. Frank N. Merrill, for appraising damage
to domestic animals, year 1900 . . . 1.00

$11.00

BREAKING ROADS.

1901.

Feb. 15. Ernest H. Goodwin, for breaking roads
in winter of 1899 and 1900 . . . . . $826.19

RECAPITULATION.

Amount charged to treasurer $15,304.43
Outstanding orders and interest $2,541.75
Miscellaneous 695.38
Roads and bridges 2,067.76
Abatements 99.79

Poor of town $179.28
County poor 594.35
Aid to dedendent soldiers 139.63
Aid to dependent soldiers chargeable to
   the county 266.75
Town officers 640.43
School money for 1900 . . . . 1,448.73
Expenses of school board 130.00
School supplies 191.10
School house repairs 258.29
County tax 1,493.56
State tax 986.00
Town library 76.20
Damage to domestic animals 11.00
Breaking roads, winter of 1899 and 1900 826.19
                              ————$12,646.19
Three notes in favor of town 463.12
Cash in hands of treasurer 2,195.12

CHARLES H. GOODWIN, Treasurer.

FRANK N. MERRILL,) Selectmen
GEORGE E. PAGE,   }   of
STEPHEN L. WEEKS,) Gilmanton.

We, the undersigned, have carefully examined the foregoing accounts and find them correctly cast and properly vouched and a balance in hands of the treasurer of $2,658.24

G. C. PARSONS,) Auditors.
H. J. MARSH,   }

LIABILITIES OF TOWN FEB. 15, 1901.

		Int.
Sarah A. Cotton	$100.00	.36
M. M. Lougee	40.00	.15
Mary Nelson	280.00	1.03
Laura F. Edgerly	170.00	4.69
N. Hodgdon	80.00	4.80
M. A. Hurd	300.00	18.00
A. M. Hurd	93.43	2.37
D. G. Edgerly	200.00	.73
A. M. Hurd	40.00	.77
M. R. Lougee	30.00	2.09
M. B. Avery	116.00	.42
M. L. Dow	121.14	.14
Vona Ham	100.00	1.26
M. A. Lougee, 5 orders	654.27	53.62
J. Young	385.93	30.57
The Bearer	417.81	25.06
Carl Smith	5.00	.49
Sarah A. Cotton	350.00	1.28
Mary B. Cook	400.00	7.67
Bertha Cook	100.00	1.92
J. H. Cook	85.00	1.63
Mary J. Potter	50.00	.18
Hannah T. Edgerly	150.00	.55
D. G. Edgerly	150.00	.55
M. A. Hurd	100.00	5.06
E. S. Nelson	200.00	.73
Mary A. Nelson	100.00	.37
Clara H. Elkins	15.00	.70
Cora B. Elkins	50.00	.18
Vona H. Paige	50.00	.18
John H. Paige	11.00	.51
Sylvia Weeks	100.00	.37
Walter C. Perkins	10.00	.45
Trustee Highland Lodge	259.09	12.00

George E. Page	$25.00	.09
Mary J. Potter	50.00	.18
Nehemiah Durgin	500.00	3.17
E. H. Goodwin	1,100.00	6.51
Clere H. Elkins	15.00	.51
David. G. Edgerly	500.00	1.83
Hannah T. Edgerly	100.00	.36
Lucy A. Young	100.00	.36
Gertrude N. Kimball	300.00	1.08
Trustee Highland Lodge No. 93, I. O. O. F.	26.40	1.09
No. 93, I. O. O. F.	173.60	7.16
Fred S. Giles	25.28	1.58
David G. Edgerly	100.00	1 88
Roy C. Edgerly	100.00	1.88
Hannah T. Edgerly	125.00	2.35
Ann T. Shannon	200.00	3.76
Charles H. Tebbetts	100.00	1.61
Irena A. Goodwin	100.00	1.86
Irena A. Goodwin	300.00	4.20
	$9,253.95	$212.34

Amount of outstanding orders and interest due Feb. 15, 1901 . . . . $9,466.29

ASSETS OF THE TOWN

Cash in hands of treasurer $2,658.24
Due from the county 81.30
                                  ————$2,739.54

                                       $6,726.75
Indebtedness over means, Feb. 15, 1900 . $8,145.27
Indebtedness over means, Feb. 15, 1901 . 6,726.75

Reduction of debt in 1900 . . . . $1,418.52

DULE OF TOWN PROPERTY.

. . . .	$18.00
. . . .	300.00
ines	250.00
for town	100.00
	$668.00

FRANK N. MERRILL, } Selectmen of
GEORGE E. PAGE, } Gilmanton.

G. E. PARSONS, } Auditors.
H. J. MARSH, }

REPORT OF SCHOOL BOARD.

To the citizens of the town of Gilmanton the School Board respectfully submit their annual report:

The number of schools supported the past year has been twelve. Whole number of pupils attending not less than two weeks, 203; boys, 104; girls, 99.

An inspection of the District at the opening of the year, showed that pupils could be best centered and schools taught in the following buildings: Kelley, Potter, Page Hill, Smith Meeting House, Lougeetown, Allen's Mills, Corner, Sanborn, Gale, Griffin, Rogers and Iron Works. Number of different teachers employed during the year has been seventeen, one male and sixteen females. For further information in regard to teachers, studies, attendance, etc., we refer you to the statistical table.

It is perhaps known to most of the citizens of the town that in order to avail ourselves of the benefits of the Literary Fund, the laws of '97 session require that all towns must support at least twenty weeks of school during the year. Not enough money was raised at your last annual meeting for school purposes to do this, therefore we find that with the strictest economy we have not been able to quite make both ends meet.

The amount of money raised for school purpose in town for several years past, has been entirely inadequate for the needs of the schools. The matter of a few hundred dollars means very little to each tax-payer, while the value of it to our girls and boys from year to year, will be more than can be well estimated. Your children have the right to demand the best you can afford to give them, to help fit them for the life work before them. Economy in the management of our town affairs is commendable, but it should not be extended to educational interests to their detriment. With the present allowance for school purposes. We find ourselves unable to compete successfully with the neighboring towns, where from twenty-five to thirty weeks of school are maintained each year; and the result is that many of our best teachers find employment where they not only receive larger salaries, but are furnished with much longer terms of school. With all due respect we would urge upon all the necessity of giving this matter your careful consideration. In reviewing the school work of the past year, we find much to encourage us to enter upon the labors of the coming year cheerfully. Our schools as a whole have been very successful. Earnest faithful work has been done by a majority of teachers and pupils. Parents and citizens have manifested a lively interest in school work. This we deem one of the best signs of the times. We must have a hearty co-operation of parents and teachers or our labors will to a certain extent be in vain.

Let your children know that you are laboring with their teacher for their highest good. Teach them respect for the "Powers that be" and their chances for gaining book knowledge will be doubled.

We have deemed it expedient to introduce new grammars thoroughout the town, hoping to create an interest in this important study, which it was not possible to do with the old text-books. We would urge upon all the importance of constant attendance upon all school duties. The record of attendance in some schools for the past year was very gratifying, while in others there is room for great improvement.

At your last annual meeting the sum of $300 was appropriated for repairs on school buildings. It was thought, at that time, by the school board, that the proper course to pursue would be to move the Griffin building to what seemed then to be a more central location ; so as to accommodate the scholars in both the Griffin and Jones Mills districts. But upon a more careful investigation it was found that the scholars at Jones Mills could be just as well accommodated by sending a part of them to Allens Mills, and the remainder to the Griffin building where it now stands.

Therefore the Griffin building was repaired on the old site, at an expense of $180. New floors were laid throughout. New doors were hung, the entire building newly plastered, and the old seats were replaced by new ones, of the O. D. Case system of seating. The interior of this building now presents a very attractive appearance.

LAURA E. VARNEY,) School Board
FRANK N. MERRILL, } of
C. FRANK PAGE,) Gilmanton

Gilmanton, N. H., Feb. 28, 1901.

ROLL OF HONOR.

KELLEY DISTRICT.—First Term—Albert H. Parsons, Alice L. Kelley, Flora H. Parsons, Ina L. Linscott, Helen L. Merrill. Worthy of Mention—Charles G. Kelley, Arthur E. Kelley, Zella A. Kelley, Ines A. Osborne.

Second Term—Ethel M. Brown, Ina S. Linscott, Flora H. Parsons. Worthy of Mention—Annie M. Lawry, Alilico E. Linscott, Zilla A. Parsons.

POTTER DISTRICT.—First Term—Eva M. Straw, Eva M. Glines, Florence M. Potter, Clara Elkins, Gladys M. Eaton, George B. Webster, Willie C. Webster, George D. Potter, John H. Page. Worthy of Mention—Grace E. Foss, Anna Foster, Robert Zanes.

Second Term—Clara Elkins, Annie Foster, Eva Glines, Florence Potter, John Page. Worthy of Mention—Eva M. Straw, Fred R. Foster, George P. Webster, Willie C. Webster, George D. Potter.

PAGE HILL DISTRICT.—First Term—R. Dorothy Collins. Worthy of Mention—Alice C. Page, Carrie B. Elkins.

SMITH MEETING HOUSE DISTRICT.—First Term—Frank J. Page, Alice M. Page, Helen M. Madera, Lamal York. Worthy of Mention—Gladys Plummer.

Second Term—Frank J. Page, Helen M. Madera.

LOUGEETOWN DISTRICT.—First Term—Cecil Lougee.

ALLENS MILLS DISTRICT.—Second Term—Alice Greenough, Melvin Greenough.

CORNER DISTRICT.—First Term—Addie Battis, Elizabeth J. Haskell, Ida Smith, Florence Wight, Harry Twombly. Worthy of Mention—Martha Munsey, John Munsey, Blanche Adams, Addie Evans, Maud Haskell.

Second Term—Blanche Adams, Martha Munsey, Ida Smith, Emily Jones. Worthy of Mention—Harry Twombly, Charlie Twombly, Addie Evans.

ROGERS DISTRICT.—First Term—Nettie Ellsworth, Ruby J. Ellsworth.

SANBORN DISTRICT.—First Term—Edith G. Batchelder, Oscar A. Ellis. Second Term—Edith G. Batchelder, Hazel B. Batchelder.

GALE DISTRICT.—First Term—Hattie B. Page, Walter J. Avery. Worthy of Mention—Ethel M. Merrill. Second Term—Charlie Lougee, Hallie B. Page.

GRIFFIN DISTRICT.—First Term—Florence Mansfield. Third Term—Margarette Pierce.

IRON WORKS.—First Term—Neil L. Jones, Paul M. Mayhew, Rosco C. Nelson, Augusta M. Foss, Marguerite A. Nelson, Mildred Place, Francis Price. Worthy of Mention—Earl Blackstone, Carl T. Smith, Willie H. Shea, Morton E. Young, Edna J. Tibbetts. Second Term—Augusta M. Foss, Neil L. Jones. Worthy of Mention—Bertha M. Emerson, Marguerite A. Nelson, S. Francis Price, Elizabeth M. Price, Walter J. Guy, Rosco C. Nelson, Harold C. Sleeper.

STATISTICAL TABLE.

No. and Name of School.	Terms.	Name of Teacher.	Wages per Month.	Length of School in Wks.	Whole No. Scholars.	Average Attendance.	Number of Scholars Attending to the following Studies.									
							Reading.	Spelling.	Penmanship.	Arithmetic.	Geography.	Grammar.	History.	Algebra.	Book Keeping.	Phys. and Hygiene.
1 Kelley	Spring	E. E. Wakefield	24	8	26	24	26	26	20	26	19	26	10	2	...	26
	Fall	Florence E. Damon	24	12	25	23	25	25	25	20	15	7	...	2	...	25
2 Potter	Spring	Effie Prescott	22	12	15	15	15	15	15	15	13	3	8	2	...	1
	Fall	Carrie E. Leyland	20	8	17	15	17	17	17	17	11	3	4	2	...	12
3 Page Hill	Spring	Bertha Jones	20	8	14	14	14	14	14	14	11	7	6	8	1	...	...
	Fall	Eva G. Osborne	22	12	15	15	15	15	15	15	11	4	5	9	1	5	6
5 Smith Meeting House	Spring	Grace G. Berry	20	8	10	10	10	10	10	10	10	8	4	...	1	...	4
	Fall	Grace G Berry	20	12	13	13	13	13	13	13	12	7	10	7	1	...	9
7 Lougeetown	Spring	Lena R. Parsons	20	8	4	4	4	4	4	4	4	3	3	...	...	1
	Fall	Lena R. Parsons	20	12	5	5	5	5	5	4	3	3	2	2	...	3
8 Allen's Mills	Spring	S. L. Batchelder	20	8	14	14	14	10	10	10	4	5	2	1	1	...
	Fall	Wm. J. Batchelder	20	12	15	11	15	15	15	15	4	4	1	...	...	4
9 Corner	Spring	Mary A. McGuire	24	8	30	28	30	30	30	30	17	16	1	...	3	30
	Fall	Mary A. Wight	24	12	28	27	28	28	28	28	26	11	9	3	4	28
10 Rogers	Spring	Eva G. Osborne	20	8	8	8	8	8	8	8	8	4	4	4	1	...	4
	Fall	Mary A. McGuire	20	12	9	9	9	9	9	9	9	4	5	4	1	...	9
11 Sanborn	Spring	Florence E. Damon	20	8	7	7	7	7	7	7	7	4	2	3	...	...	7
	Fall	L. Bell Smith	20	12	7	7	7	7	7	7	7	5	3	3	...	...	
12 Gale	Spring	R. Esther Toas	24	8	8	7	8	8	8	8	6	6	4	...	...	2
	Fall	Ava Weare	22	12	9	9	9	9	9	9	8	7	6	.	2	...	...
14 Griffin	Spring	Ethel Pease	20	8	11	10	11	11	10	9	3	1	...	...	...	6
	Fall	Ethel Pease	20	11	13	10	13	13	10	10	2	3	1	1	...	...
15 Iron Works	Spring	Edith M. Page	24	8	21	20	21	21	21	19	11	5	5	...	...	...
	Fall	Edith M. Page	24	12	20	20	20	20	20	18	6	6	6	...	...	...

Other studies attended to during the year : Composition, 42; Civil Government, 8; Drawing, 44; Botany, 48; Phy., 1; Vocal Music, 65.

TREASURER'S REPORT.

Amount charged to treasurer for support of schools		$1,468.16
Required by law	$1,284.96	
Literary fund	119.70	
Balance of dog license	43.10	
From town of Alton tuition	29.00	
From Mrs. Varney chalk sold	.40	
		$1,468.16

Cr.

By amount paid for miscellaneous	$108.79	
Teachers' salaries, summer term	516.00	
Teachers' salaries, fall term	788.00	
Deficit 1899	54 97	
		$1,467.76

Balance in hands of treasurer	.40

MISCELLANEOUS.

1900.

Mar.	22.	The Johnson Co., incidentals	$4.97
June	21.	George W. Griffin, for wood	4.67
	25.	Laura E Varney, incidentals	1.69
	25.	Mrs. Jay Munsey, transportation of Merrill boy	3.00
	25.	Laura E. Varney, cash paid for cleaning Sanborn and Rogers school houses .	2.00
	26.	Mrs. S. M. Hayes, cleaning Kelly school house	2.00
	26.	C. Frank Page, cash paid for supplies .	2.65
Aug.	17.	John S. Page, for one cord wood fitted .	4.00
	17.	C. Frank Page, for wood and fitting same, Gale district	4.00
Oct.	9.	John L. Clifford, transporting scholars from Jones' Mills to Allen's Mills .	8.00
	23.	Romie Little, one cord wood furnished Roger's district	3.75

Nov.	22.	Laura E. Varney, cash paid for pens, brooms, pail, etc.	$2.46
	24.	Ushers Parsons, for wood furnished Kelley district	3.00
Dec.	1.	Herman A. Page, wood furnished Iron Works' district	2.60
	6.	Geo. W. Dow 2nd, for wood furnished Corner district	4.00
	15.	Elmer L. Green, carrying scholars to Griffin school	18.00
	20.	Herbert A. Sargent, for carrying scholars to Sanborn school	20.00
Jan.	26.	Mrs. Jennie Clifford, for transportion of scholars to Allen's Mills' school . . .	12.00
	26.	H. W. Downing, wood furnished Allen's Mills' school	2.00
	26.	Henry E. Page, wood furnished Page Hill school	4.00

$108.79

SCHOOL HOUSE REPAIRS.

1900.

Amount charged to treasurer for school house repairs	$259.26
Whole amount expended	213.84

Balance in hands of treasurer	$45.42

June	25.	Laura E. Varney for cash paid for repairs on Rogers school house	4.30
	26.	George E. Page for repairing Smith Meeting house school house	2.50
Aug.	17.	Fred V. Pease, for labor and lumber, Griffin school house	2.00
Oct.	9.	H. A. Maxfield, for cash paid for lime and drawing lumber for Griffin school house	12.03

Oct.	9.	John W. Ham, labor plastering Griffin school house	$7.00
	9.	Mrs. C. A. Twombly, for cleaning Griffin school house	1.00
	27.	Laconia Lumber Co., for lumber for Griffin building	27.63
Nov.	6.	Augustus Pierce, for labor on Griffin building	1.25
	6.	Herman A. Page, for labor on Griffin school house	11.44
	7.	C. Frank Page, for labor on Griffin building	16.87
	7..	C. Frank Page, for material furnished Griffin building	7.46
	7.	C. F. Page, for desks and curtains furnished Griffin building	9.85
	7.	William Tilton, repairing stove Griffin building	2.17
	7.	J. W. Follett, for paper, etc	1.90
	22.	Frank Varney, repairing Sanborn school house	1.55
	24.	F. N. Merrill, cash paid for nails, catches and door knobs, etc., furnished Griffin building	4.19
	24.	F. N. Merrill, for labor repairing Griffin building	14.50
Dec.	6.	John S. Beck, repairing Sanborn building,	2.48
	29.	John P. Hussey, for lumber and steps .	5.77
	29.	O. D. Case & Co., for seats and desks for Griffin building	61.45
	26.	Harry Mudgett, repairing Allens Mills building	.50
Feb.	15.	Asa F. Page, painting Page Hill building two coats	9.00
	15.	Asa F. Page, painting Lougeetown building two coats	7.00

$213.84

SUMMER SCHOOLS.

1900.

June 25. Eva G. Osborn, teaching, eight weeks, in
Rogers' district $40.00

25. Mrs. Sarah Batchelder, teaching eight
weeks in Allen's Mills' district . . . 40.00

25. Florence Damon, teaching eight weeks in
Sanborn district 40.00

25. Electa E. Wakefield, teaching eight weeks
in Kelley district 48.00

25. Ethel Pease, teaching eight weeks in
Griffin district 40.00

25. Effie Prescott, teaching eight weeks in
Potter district 40.00

25. Grace G. Berry, teaching eight weeks in
Smith Meeting House district . . . 40.00

25. Mary A. McGuire, teaching eight weeks
in Corner district 48.00

29. Bertha Jones, for teaching eight weeks in
Page Hill district 44.00

29. Rachel Esther Toas, for teaching eight
weeks in Gale district 48.00

July 6. Edith M. Page, for teaching eight weeks
in Iron Works' district 48.00

6. Lena R. Parsons, for teaching eight weeks
in Lougeetown district 40.00

_____

$516.00

FALL SCHOOLS.

Nov. 6. Daniel Moulton, for tuition of Moulton
child nineteen weeks $19.00

22. Belle Smith, teaching twelve weeks in
Sanborn district 60.00

22. Mary A. McGuire, teaching twelve
weeks in Rogers district 60.00

22. William Batchelder, teaching twelve
weeks in Allens Mills district 60.00

Nov. 22. Mary A. Wight, teaching twelve weeks
              in Corner district $72.00

       22. Florence E. Damon, teaching twelve weeks
              in Kelley district 72.00

       22. Grace Berry, teaching twelve weeks in
              Smith Meeting House district 60.00

       26. Mrs. Carrie Leyland for teaching twelve
              weeks in Potter district 66.00

       28. Eva G. Osborn, teaching twelve weeks in
              Page Hill district 66.00

       30. Lena R. Parsons, teaching twelve weeks
              in Lougeetown district 60.00

Dec.   3. Ava J. Weare, teaching twelve weeks in
              Gale district 66.00

        8. Edith M. Page, teaching twelve weeks in
              Iron Works' district 72.00

       14. Ethel Pease, teaching twelve weeks in
              Griffin district 55.00
                                                        ———
                                                        $788.00

CHARLES H. GOODWIN, Treasurer.

GEORGE C. PARSONS, ⎫
HERBERT J. MARSH,   ⎬ Auditors.
                    ⎭

Births Registered in the Town of Gilmanton for the Year Ending December 31, 19—

Date of Birth	Name of Child. [if any.]	Male or Female.	Living or Stillborn.	No. Child.	Color.	Name of Father.	Maiden Name of Mother.	Color.	Residence of Parents.	Occupation of Father.	Birthplace of Father.	Birthplace of Mother.
Feb. 26	Geo. Henry Jones	M.	Living	3	w	C. Fred Potter	Andena M. Diamond	w	Gilmanton	Farmer	Gilmanton	London
Mar. 17	Albert E. Page	M.	"	8	"	Geo A. J...	Olive E. Speare	"	"	Farmer	"	Canterbury
" 19		M.	"	1	"	Henry E. Page	Ida A. Pendergast	"	"	Farmer	"	Barnstead
Apr. 18	Edna Page	F.	"	4	"	Jender Hilliard	Ellen	"	"	Pedler	"	Sutton Me...
" 27	Flossie Hill	F.	"	2	"	Wm E. Page	Cora E. Couch	"	"	Pedler	"	
May 2		F.	"	1	"	Elwood Hill	Ella My Dame	"	"	Farmer	"	i
" 3		F.	"	3	"	Alfred M. Brown	Edna Ash	"	"	Farmer	Epsom	Belmont
Jne 5	Carrie E. Jones	F.	"	1	"	Jae C. Jones	Ellin E. Brown	"	"		Epsom	Nova Scotia
Aug. 25		F.	"	1	"	Edwin S. Brown	Mry E. Walsh	"	"	Laborer		Epsom
" 14	Elva C. Little	M.	"	4	"	Ervin C. Brock	Kae L. Fot	"	"	Laborer	Pittsfield	
Nov. 28	Wm. Silsby Weeks	M.	"	1	"	Romie Little	Ula M. Beaman	"	"	Farmer	Pittsfield	Lynn, Mass
" 15		F.	"	1	"	Lorrain E. Weeks	Ade E. Net	"	"	Farmer	Ohio, Mass	Lakeport
Dec. 2		M.	"	2	"	Mr F. Ellsworth	Alice A.	"	"	Farmer		Waterford
" 6		M.	"	1	"	Mt L. Lyster	Jennie B. Lyster	"	"	Butter Maker	Ga...	Mch
" 21	Eva Gertrude Smith	F.	"	1	"	J. Mr Smith	Edith L. Hannaford	"	"	Farmer		Mch

I hereby certify that the above return is correct, according to the best of my knowledge and belief.

Roy C. EDGERLY, Town Clerk.

Marriages Registered in the Town of Gilmanton for the Year Ending Dec. 31, 1900.

Place of Marriage	Name and Surname of Groom and Bride	Residence of Each at time of Marriage	Age of Each	Color of Each	Occupation of Groom and Bride	Place of Birth of Each	Names of Parents	Birthplace of Parents	Occupation	Marriage	Name, Residence and Official Station of Person by Whom Married
Laconia	Scott A. Kimball	Belmont	29	All White	Farmer	Belmont	Jerem'h S. Kimball / Lavina F. Sanborn	Belmont	Housewife	1	J. E. Everingham, Clergyman, Laconia.
	Myrtie B. Smith	Gilmanton	24	"	Housemaid	Gilmanton	Edward E. Smith / Jane Evans	Gilmanton, "	Laborer	1	
Gilmanton	Lyman E. Berry	"	36	"	Farmer	New Durham	Eben E. Berry / Lucy M. Chesley	New Durham, "	Housewife	3	John H. Wilkins, Gilmanton.
	Lulu M. Foss	"	22	"	Housemaid	Danvers, Ms.	John C. Foss / Ella M. Watson	Gilmanton / Alton	Farmer	1	
Gilmanton	Charles W. Ordway	"	29	"	Teamster	Plymouth	Willard Ordway / Sarah Locke		Housewife	1	N. B. McMurphy, Clergyman, Gilmanton.
	Hattie F. Maxfield	"	29	"	Shoemaker	Gilmanton	John A. Maxfield / Aphia Page	Gilmanton	Shoemaker	1	
Gilmanton	Edwin S. Barron	"	31	"	Farmer	Belmont	George Barron		Housewife	1	Royal McDonald, Clergyman, Gilmanton.
	Mary E. Walsh	"	20	"	Housekeeper	Nova Scotia	Smith Walsh			1	
Alton	Seldon B. Rollins	"	25	"	Farmer	Gilmanton	E. B. Rollins		Housek'pr	1	N. A. Avery, Clergyman, Alton.
	Alma L. Ellis	"	20	"	Housekeeper	Alton	Mary L. Sargent / Elbridge Ellis		Farmer	1	
Barnstead	Charles T. Brock	"	31	"	Farmer	Pittsfield	John B. Brock		Farmer	1	Lewis Elkins, Clergyman, Barnstead.
	Carrie L. Roby	"	31	"	Housekeeper	Epsom	Orrin Dowst / Martha Griffin			2	
London	Herbert W. Downing	"	25	"	Farmer	Gilmanton	L. W. Downing / Martha Webber	Gilmanton	Farmer	1	James McLaughlin, Clergyman.
	Margaret A. McLeod	London	24	"	Dressmaker	P. E. Island	James McLeod / Mary McLaughlin			1	

Town	Name	Residence	Occupation	Age	Race	Parent	Parent Birthplace	Occupation	No.	Officiant
lmanton	William S. P. Sanderson	Gilmanton,	Druggist	37	All White	C. S P. Sanderson	Gilmanton	Druggist	1	Mark A. Roberts, Clergyman, Gilmanton.
	Florence E. Hoyt	"	Housewife	33		Anna J. Mack	Manchester	Housewife	1	
						George A. Hoyt	Loudon	Painter		
						Letitia D. Hoyt	Meredith	Dr'ssma'er	2	
lmanton	John W. Swain	"	Farmer	63		John L. Swain	Gilmanton	Farmer	3	John H. Wilkins, Clergyman, Gilmanton.
	Francis Durrell	"	Housewife	71		Olive Batchelder		Housewite		
						Samuel Batchelder	Alton	Staged'ver		
						Sally Clark		Housewife	2	
lmanton	Herbert N. Weeks	"	Farmer	40		Noah Weeks	"	Farmer	2	Amos B. Russell, Clergyman, Laconia.
	Lilla M. Benitez	"	Housewife	27		Sarah A. McNeal		Housewife		
						Agustus Durgin	Thornton	Farmer		
						Anna P Sanborn	"	Housewife	1	
lmanton	Frank W. Foss	"	Farmer	24		Charles W. Foss	Deerfield	Farmer	1	Royal McDonald, Clergyman, Gilmanton.
	Nettie R. Peaslee	"	Housekeeper	22		Lucy J. Marsh	Gilmanton	Housewife		
						Caleb W. J. Peaslee	"	Farmer		
						Luanna M. Abbott	Warner	Housewife	1	
lmanton	Wilard G. McClary	"	Teamster	34		Joseph B. McClary		Farmer	1	Royal McDonald, Clergyman, Gilmanton.
	Dorothy Butcher	Pittsfield	Housekeeper	18		Frances A. Adams	Bristol	Housek'pr		
						Edward Butcher	Germanton, Pa,	Carpenter	1	
						Lydia Bardeen	Dover	Housek'pr		
ffstown	Robert A. Whitehouse	Manchester	Farmer	21		E. B. Whitehouse	Middleton	Carpenter	1	Hen'y H. Wentworth. Goffstown.
	Nellie C. Page	Gilmanton	Housekeeper	22		M. E. Brown	Trov, Vt.	Farmer		
						Dixi C. Page	Gilmanton	Farmer	1	
						Cyrena Webster	"	Housewife		
lmanton	J. Wilbur Smith	"	Farmer	32		Charles T. Smith	"	Farmer	3	Royal McDonald, Clergyman, Gilmanton.
	Edith L. Hannaford	"	Housekeeper	20		Eva J. Foss	New York	Housek'pr		
						T. F. Hannaford	New York	Bro'm Mf'g		
						Louise Landon	Vermont	Housek'pr	1	

hereby certify that the above return is correct, according to the best of my knowledge and belief.

ROY C. EDGERLY, Town Clerk.

Date of Death	Name and Surname of the Deceased	Age Years	Months	Days	Place of Birth	Sex	Color	Single, Marr'd or Widowed	Occupation	Place of Birth Father	Place of Birth Mother	Name of Father	Name of Mother
Mr. 25	Ms. Wm	75			Alton	†		M	H	Std		Sin Foss	Lucy
Mr. 28	J ne	73	1	117	Barnstead	†		S	ife	nd		Tns east	Bets
Apr. 2	hn (bg	82			Gilmanton	†		W	nd	nd		David S. Young	
Apr. 4	Mark A. Dennett	30	1	18	Gilmanton	†	All White	S	Farmer				
Apr. 10	yMie E.	74	10	28		†		M	nfer	nd		Riley M. B flord	
Apr. 17	Mn thr	74	11	8	Gilmanton	†		M					Euni
Apr. 28	nas P. Mh	80			Sheffield	†		M	dn	Gin		David El vth	Mar
June 6	Dr. R. M. Gray	37	5			†		S	Farmer		Std		Ge Gay	Mar
July 6	Willis dddy	20	10	7	Nova Scotia	†		M	Me	Me	N Ova Scotia		Mar ody	Sara
July 13	Mry E. en	16		519	Chel ea. Mass.	†		M	Girl	Gin		A. S. Vith	Harr
July 19	te M. Marsh	54	10	8	Banett, Vt.	†		M	Me	th. Vt.	Willi		dew Marsh	Harr
Aug. 16	Harriet M. Mgt	61	10	13	Ba nd	†		S	tter	nd	Lee		Nkiah Ms.	Sobr
Sept. 21	Sa Edgerly	81			Oldtown, Me.	†		W	ater				Rhen E gly	
Sept. 26	Sd D. Varney	68	4	6	Newb'ry't, Mass	†		W	Me	Mt, Mass				Joan
Nov. 10	L. Jane Thompson	85	5	13	ton	†		W		Gin	Lakeport		as Pettingell	Alice
Nov. 22	Mary L. Short			1	G	†		S					Mr H. Ellsworth	Melv
Dec. 2					Pittsfield	†		S					John C. Gault	Beli
Dec. 5	Elt	23	1	3	Gilmanton	†		S		B nd			D il	
Dec. 12	Em G. Goodwin		7			†		M	Farmer		Gilmanton		Gn	
Dec. 22	as R. Price	79				†							William ce	

†Female.   † Me.

I   by certify that the above return is   ect,   ding to the   bst of my knowledge   ad   lif.

       Roy C.   Ev, Town